Disrupting Time
Sermons, Prayers, and Sundries

by

Stanley Hauerwas

Cascade Books
A division of *Wipf & Stock Publishers*
199 West 8th Avenue, Suite 3 • Eugene OR 97401

Cascade Books
A division of Wipf & Stock Publishers
199 West 8th Avenue, Suite 3
Eugene, OR 97401

Disrupting Time
Sermons, Prayers, and Sundries
Copyright©2004 by Stanley Hauerwas
ISBN: 1-59244-939-5
Publication Date: October 2004

to
Kendall Boynton Hauerwas

Contents

Foreword 3

Introduction 5

Sermons and Prayers
I. Aldersgate Sermons 17
   1. The Hastening that Waits 19
   2. Like Those Who Dream 29
   3. Jews and the Eucharist 39
   4. God and the Fourth of July 47
   5. Christ the King 58
   6. Heirs, by Paula Gilbert 67

II. From Bennettsville, South Carolina to Scotland and Chapel Hill, North Carolina 71
   1. Witnesses Against Ourselves 73
   2. Providential Peace 83
   3. Boasting in the Third Heaven 93
   4. The Good Samaritan: An Expository Sermon 100

III. Marriage Sermons 107
   1. How the Virgin Birth Makes Marriage Possible 109
   2. An Apocalyptic Marriage 113
   3. Rightly Dressed 117

IV. The Ministry and Other Callings 129
   1. For the Love of Ministry 131
   2. Sacrificing Priests 137
   3. On Milk and Jesus 142

V. Two Remembrances: John Howard Yoder and Tommy Langford 161

VI. Hauerwas on Hauerwas: Interviews 169
   1. With the *Zion Herald* (Stephen Swecker) 171
   2. With *Duke Magazine* (William Cavenaugh) 180
   3. With *Image* (Brian Volck) 189
   4. With *Cross Currents* (Michael Quirk) 204

VII. Sundries 219
   1. On Being a Theologian 221
   2. Explaining Why Willimon Never Explains 224
   3. Confessions of a Mennonite Camp Follower 234

Foreword

I have long wanted to put this book of sermons and prayers together. I have done so because I wanted to dedicate a book to Paula and my second grandson, Kendall Boynton Hauerwas. Kendall is now almost four. Since he was born I have published several books that I could have dedicated to Kendall. But I did not want to dedicate one of my more "academic" books to Kendall. Do not misunderstand. I like my more "academic" books, but often the analysis and arguments in those books have only an indirect relation to that about which I most care.

I wanted to dedicate a book to Kendall that was like *Prayers Plainly Spoken*, the book I dedicated to our first grandson, Joel Adam Hauerwas. If Kendall ever becomes curious about his grandfather and grandmother, I hope these sermons, prayers, and interviews will help him understand what has made our lives possible. What has made our lives possible is quite simply the church of Jesus Christ. It is my hope that everything we are and do is unintelligible if the God Christians worship does not exist. So I hope this book will help Kendall someday have a sense of the loves that make us what we are.

Friends, of course, also make me what I am. One of those friends is Jon Stock. I met Jon fifteen years ago through the Church of the Servant King. There is one terribly ugly reality that has always made our friendship difficult—Jon is a Yankee fan. Even worse he is devoid of any shame for supporting the rightly despised Yankees. However, Jon loves God and books. I do not know if it is quite right to say Jon runs the bookstore in Eugene, because he fortunately can count on the responsible people surrounding him. But by some stroke of fortune he is now running the publishing firm that has produced this book. I am extremely pleased to be published by Cascade, if for no other reason than to remind Jon that Kendall will be brought up right—a Red Sox fan.

Tristin Hassell and Matthew Olver have helped me put this book together. I am extremely fortunate that students come my way wanting to help me do what I do. I only hope that they will learn better how to do what I do as part of that process. Alex Sider has not only been a graduate student (now graduated) but also a good friend. I am indebted to him for helping to make this a better book. As usual, Sarah Freedman did the work necessary to give this book life. Only Sarah knows how much I owe her.

For anyone kind enough to read this book I want to say "thank you." I know I write a great deal. I not only write a great deal, but I publish what I write. I not only publish what I write, but I often publish what I write in multiple venues. I do not think everything I write needs to be published, but as Paula recently pointed out, at this stage in my life everything I do will be read by someone, so I might as well get it out on my terms. I am aware that some of those "someones" read most of what I write. For those "someones" reading this book I can only say, "Thank you." I hope you will enjoy this book as much as I enjoyed writing and bringing together these sermons, prayers, and sundries.

Introduction

I. The Time That Is Disrupted

Americans believe we live in a disrupted time. September 11, 2001 disrupted American time. Thus, we are told time after time September 11, 2001 has forever changed our lives. *Disrupting Time*, however, is not about September 11, 2001. *Disrupting Time* is about the disruption of time by a time named Jesus. Thus my contention that Christians do not believe that September 11, 2001 changed the world because the world was changed in 33 A.D.[1] We, that is, Christians believe we can only know what happened on September 11, 2001 because God acted decisively on behalf of the world in 33 A.D.

What happened in 33 A.D. was a disruption in time that reconstituted time. Jesus' life, death, resurrection, and the subsequent birth of the church forever changed how we must think of time.[2] Christian time is apocalyptic

---

[1] For my reflections on September 11, 2001, see the essay, "September 11, 2001: A Pacifist Response," and sermon, "September 11, 2001: A Sermon a Year Later," in my book, *Performing the Faith: Bonhoeffer and the Practice of Nonviolence* (Grand Rapids: Brazos Press, 2004), 201-214.

[2] I had trouble finding a title for this book, but "disrupting time" came to me once I forced myself to acknowledge the apocalyptic character of these sermons. Several days after I entitled the book I realized I had probably drawn on the title of George Hunsinger's book on Barth, *Disruptive Grace: Studies in the Theology of Karl Barth* (Grand Rapids: Eerdmans, 2000). I think on the whole what I am suggesting by the title "disrupting time" is compatible with Barth's understanding of the eschatological character of Christian convictions. Hunsinger quotes Barth: "The New Testament speaks eschatologically when

time, that is, a time that makes all things new.³ In an address before the staff, students, and patients of the Christian Medical College in Vellore, India, Lesslie Newbigin sounded the apocalyptic character of the Gospel:

> If Jesus died and rose again, then we are at the beginning of a new world, a new creation.... He is One who has always created, who is always creating, and who is moving forward with the creation to the end for which, in the beginning, He was the agent.... He is this because he is the One who not only died, who not only suffered, who has not only gone down to the depths of the human predicament, who has not only known the deepest darkness of pain and despair and defeat and death, to face them, to master them, conquer them—He is the one who goes before as the pioneer, the leader of the human march. In Jesus, in Jesus alone, the ultimate depth and height of the human situation has been measured. He is the One who alone has the keys of death and hell.⁴

It is my hope that the sermons and prayers collected in this book exemplify Newbigin's conviction that in Christ the Father has made all things new through the work of the Spirit.

I have not collected these sermons (and prayers) because I think I am an exceptional preacher. I do, however, love to preach. Often, I discover my deepest theological convictions when I am at work on a sermon. I do so, I think, because it never occurs to me when I am working on a sermon that I am trying to "defend a position." Of course, that may be because I have never had a position to defend. I am probably not smart enough to

---

it speaks of humanity's being called, reconciled, justified, sanctified and redeemed. In speaking thus it speaks really and properly. One has to realize that God is the measure of all that is real and proper, that eternity comes first and then time, and therefore the future comes first and then the present" (174, cf. Barth, *Church Dogmatics*, I.1, 464). I fully agree with Barth, so long as the eternity/time relation is not understood in neo-Kantian fashion.

³In his book, *Paul Among the Postliberals: Pauline Theology Beyond Christendom and Modernity* (Grand Rapids: Brazos Press, 2003), Douglas Harink provides an extremely interesting account of contemporary theological proposals in the light of Paul's eschatology.

⁴Geoffrey Wainwright uses this quote in his "Heresy Then and Now: Reflections on a Treatise of Tertullian," *Pro Ecclesia* 8: 2 (Spring, 2004): 224-225.

have a position to defend, but it is also the case that I do not believe theologians should have "positions." Our task is to help the church live the story we have been given.

When I preach, or at least when I am writing a sermon, I have a sense of freedom and joy that I hope is contagious. "Contagious," of course, is often seen negatively as the passing on of an infection. No doubt, to be infected with the good news that is Christ can and should make us feel as if we have "caught something." We have, of course, "been caught," forcing us to recognize that life will never be the same. I hope, therefore, that those kind enough to read these sermons, prayers, and interviews will laugh from time to time as they read, because I think humor is correlative to an apocalyptic perspective. If we did not laugh and cry at the incongruities we discover and recognize when faced by the Gospel, then we would have a sign that we are far too serious to be Christian.

I cannot pretend that I have any thing so grand as a homiletical strategy or theory.[5] I hope, however, that I have developed habits, theological habits, that shape how I preach. Others may well be able to articulate those habits on my behalf better than I am able to do, but in general I think I approach each sermon determined to help us see what can only be seen by attending to how these texts make us see what otherwise would go unnoticed. In short, I try to locate the extraordinary world in which we live if in fact Jesus is who the church proclaims him to be.

I assume that most Christians live as I live, that is, finding it hard on a daily basis to live in God's time. "The normal" is so tempting. We normally assume, for example, that if we are to survive someone needs to protect us with guns. But the apocalyptic character of the Gospel defies that "normal." How extraordinary. So, I find my life interrupted Sunday after Sunday by the sermon. I try to return the favor when I preach. I do so because I know that having my life disrupted by the gospel makes me happy. After all, what we have to proclaim is "good news."

---

[5] I have learned a great deal about how to think about preaching from my colleague, Richard Lischer, and my friend and former student, Charles Campbell. In particular see Campbell's *Preaching Jesus: New Directions for Homiletics in Hans Frei's Postliberal Theology* (Grand Rapids: Eerdmans, 1997). Of course, Will Willimon has probably taught me more than anyone. The essay that ends this book I hope not only illumines Will's preaching, but also the sermons in this book.

"Paradox" is a word I seldom use. But I believe the apocalyptic character of the Gospel paradoxically makes possible the everyday. Because time has been redeemed we have time to marry, have children, feed the hungry, enjoy singing, be friends, and worship God. If I try to do anything in my sermons it is to help us see and make connections between the everyday and what God has done in Christ. Of course, if the sermon "works" it often means that the everyday feels quite odd, but to live on God's time cannot help but make us odd.

By collecting these sermons and prayers I hope to counter two criticisms made of my work. I have often been criticized for my inattention to scripture, or at least I have been accused of failing to be appropriately textual. That I have been so criticized is very much my own fault, given the argument of *Unleashing the Scripture: Freeing the Bible from Captivity to America*.[6] My good colleague and friend, Richard Hays, notes that my interpretations of biblical texts rarely depend on detailed exegesis or sustained close reading.[7] Hays is surely correct that I often do not expose how I have come to read the text as I have, but I do think the words of the text matter.[8] I would like to think that these sermons show why I think it very dangerous to use the scripture to support some prior determined "idea." So, I try very hard in these sermons, as well as the sermons in *Unleashing the Scripture*, to be true to the texts assigned for that Sunday.

In most of my sermons I try to show the connections among all three texts. I do so because I am convinced that a Christological reading of the Old Testament is crucial if Christians are to avoid the temptation, a temptation almost unavoidable in our day, to "idealize" the Gospel. The Gospel is as concrete as flesh and blood. That my sermons and prayers struggle with the people of Israel, the Jews, reflects my conviction of the materiality of the Gospel. Accordingly, I try to make it impossible to look

---

[6] Stanley Hauerwas, *Unleashing the Scripture: Freeing the Bible from Captivity to America* (Nashville: Abingdon Press, 1993).
[7] Hays expressed these worries in *The Moral Vision of the New Testament: A Contemporary Introduction to New Testament Ethics* (New York: Harper Collins, 1996), 253-265. See especially pg. 259.
[8] Telford Work argues that scripture is constitutive of our salvation. Thus, the materiality of the text is analogous to Christ's humanity. See his *Living and Active: Scripture in the Economy of Salvation* (Grand Rapids: Eerdmans, 2002).

Introduction

for a "meaning" in the texts that is more important than the text itself.

That I believe the church is at once the witness to and reality of God's care for the world often invites the criticism that the church I say must exist does not, except as some ideal. But these sermons have been preached and, even more importantly, have been heard by Christians. Preaching is not some make-believe activity. Preaching is the most political of tasks. Preaching presupposes and forms a people. The church must exist if preaching is to be intelligible. God's word, moreover, even when it is the word of judgment, affects those that preach and those that hear. Such an "effect" takes time, but then that is what is to be expected given the disruption of time by God's time. That there exists a church that makes it possible to preach sermons—sermons that disrupt our worlds—surely suggests my church is not an ideal.

2. The Character of This Book: Sermons and Prayers

I do not think the way I have organized these sermons and prayers is arbitrary, but I have not tried to impose an order where there is none. There are connections to be made among the sermons, but I thought it made more sense to group the sermons by where they were preached rather than force them into thematic categories. The prayers that follow each of the sermons could have easily been arranged differently, but I put them where I did mainly because they seemed to "go" there.

I continue to worry about publishing prayers, but I do so because my students and friends ask me to include my prayers in what I write. I worry about publishing prayers because I think we ought to pray in a way disciplined by the prayers the church has honed through the centuries. I am, however, gratified by the many letters I received in response to *Prayers Plainly Spoken*.[9] The problem with publishing prayers is the temptation to think that you write the prayer to be published rather than to pray to God. I think it is helpful, therefore, that these prayers are interspersed with the sermons rather than standing alone. However, I have not tried to hide that most of these prayers were written to be prayed before my Christian Ethics class.

---

[9] *Prayers Plainly Spoken* is now available from Wipf and Stock publishers in Eugene, Oregon.

Disrupting Time

I often forget to date my sermons. Some of the sermons that were preached at Aldersgate United Methodist Church, the church Paula and I attended for fourteen years, were preached some years ago. I find, however, that, as I suggested above, I am certainly settled into habits that give the sermons a consistency of style and content. I suspect that many of these sermons are so similar because they were preached at Aldersgate to a people I had come to know and who had come to know me. I do not think, for example, that I would have had the necessary moral authority to have preached "God and the Fourth of July" in a church in which I was not known.

I have included Paula's sermon "Heirs" for the simple reason that I think it is such a good sermon. Moreover, since this is a book dedicated to Kendall I thought it appropriate for Kendall to discover that Paula is as implicated in this "Christian stuff" as I am. I hope, moreover, that her sermon makes clear how much I have learned from hearing her preach over the years. Paula celebrates and gives a homily every Thursday for the Wesley Fellowship at Duke. To listen to how carefully she parses the texts of scripture week after week is an inspiration for me.

The five sermons in the second grouping are what I say they are, occasional sermons preached at diverse locations. The First Presbyterian Church of Bennetsville, South Carolina is a long way from St. Salvators, Church of Scotland. The latter is also the university church of the University of St. Andrews, Scotland. I tried to preach at both churches faithfully to the text assigned for that day. I preached at Bennetsville because the Rev. Scott Andrews and I are both members of the Ekklesia Project, and he was kind enough to ask me to be the theologian in residence at his church for a few days. He is a brave man. I preached at St. Salvators during the time I was at St. Andrews to give the Gifford Lectures. I was tempted to put the sermon at the end of *With the Grain of the Universe*, but I thought I had tested the patience of my hosts at St. Andrews too much as it was.

The two sermons I preached at the Church of the Holy Family, Chapel Hill, the church where Paula and I now worship, were preached during the summer when our rector went on vacation. There are so many good preachers at Holy Family, not the least being our rector, Fr. Timothy Kimbrough, that I much prefer to be a listener than a preacher at Holy

Introduction

Family. But, when Timothy asks Paula and me to preach we do what he requests.

The marriage sermons need no explanation. Those being married were my graduate students. The names in "An Apocalyptic Marriage" have been changed because the marriage was not one made in heaven. I decided to include it, however, because in that sermon I say more exactly what I take to be the time that makes marriage possible between Christians. I confess that I like to preach at weddings between Christians, though I assume that the bride and groom are not positioned to be the most receptive hearers. But then, as I try to make clear in these sermons, the burden is not so much on them as on those who have come to witness their vows.

The last sermons are those preached at services involving ministry. "For the Love of the Ministry" was preached at Kyle Childress' tenth anniversary of his ministry at Austin Heights Baptist Church in Nacogdoches, Texas. Kyle is an old and dear friend, which means I took advantage of the situation to preach a catholic sermon to the Baptists. Kyle cannot blame it on me, however, because I could not help it that the First Thessalonians text came up in the lectionary. Rob MacSwain is also an old friend who honored me by asking me to preach his ordination. It is true that Rob was one of the aides to George Cary, the Archbishop of Canterbury, and then found himself the next year in Kinston, North Carolina. Kinston is a nice enough town, but it is a long way from London. "On Milk and Jesus" was the result of being asked to preach at the Installation of Gerald Gerbrandt to be the first president of Canadian Mennonite University. How wonderful it is that a people still exist that think there ought to be a sermon when the president of the university is installed.

I have also included at the end of this last group of sermons two "remembrances" I wrote for the memorial services of John Howard Yoder and Tommy Langford. My relation to John needs no elaboration for most who will read this book. Tommy Langford was a dear friend from Duke. I wanted to include a remembrance of Stuart Henry, but I could not find it. Stuart taught at the Divinity School for many years. He directed Paula's dissertation. He was a Presbyterian and Southern gentleman. I mention him only because he meant so much to Paula and me. Tommy Langford was a philosophical theologian who held many administrative posts at

Duke. I hope in these short "remembrances" something of their extraordinary lives comes through.

I have not followed each of the sermons in the last two parts with prayers, but rather put the prayers at the end of each of those sections. The prayers, particularly following the last section, deal with life and death. I hope the readers of those prayers will not find them morose, but rather a celebration of lives that I so deeply admire. The prayers for James McClendon, Dale Aukerman, and Dietrich Bonhoeffer, as well as the remembrances of John, Stuart, and Tommy, I hope testify to the importance of their lives for my life. I have also included prayers dealing with the deaths of children, parents, and spouses of those I love. The only reason for including these prayers is that I have been told that these prayers seem truthful.

3. Sundries

I hope that the last part of this book is self-explanatory. It consists of interviews I have given in the past few years. I include them because the informal nature of these interviews may help some understand a bit better what I am about. I have been interviewed often, but I do not think I am particularly good at being interviewed. When I read interviews with Michel Foucault, Alasdair MacIntyre, or Rowan Williams, I am humbled. They could and do speak in intelligible paragraphs. I can hardly speak in an intelligible sentence.

I begin with the interviews that are more general and move to those that are about particular aspects of my work. I was surprised to discover reading through the interviews that I did not say the same thing from one interview to the next. That I was not repetitious I am sure owes more to the questions asked than my ability to avoid saying the same thing over again. Like any academic who has been around for a long time, I have standard answers to standard questions. I do not think repetition is always a bad thing, particularly when you are challenging, as I try to do, fundamental habits of speech. But you do not want to be boring either.

I have discovered the better the interviewer the better the interview I give. So, I need to identify as well as thank those who did the interviews. Stephen Swecker is the editor of the *Zion Herald* and has single handedly

Introduction

resurrected that magazine. I admire his energy and passion for the Gospel. *Duke Magazine* was kind to bring in Bill Cavanaugh, a former student and long-standing friend, for its interview. Few know more about me than Bill. Brian Volk is a physician-poet who has been kind enough to claim me as a friend. Michael Quirk is a philosopher and long time friend. Mike does not claim to be a Christian, but few understand me better than Michael. The prayer for Eileen was for Mike's wife. I have included in this last section a brief address I gave on receiving an honorary degree from Marymount Manhattan College. I have done so because I hope it suggests my love for what I do. I love being a theologian. I love to preach. I am learning to pray. I do not know if I will ever learn to enjoy being Stanley Hauerwas. But I do know I have been given a wonderful life. I hope that these sermons and prayers in some small way embody the joy that comes from being a Christian.

I have included two essays in the Appendix that I hope help "explain" the way I preach as well as my commitment to nonviolence. I was obviously "having fun" in both of the essays, and I hope the reader will find them amusing.

Sermons and Prayers

Aldersgate Sermons

The Hastening That Waits[10]

Isaiah 40: 1-11
2 Peter 3: 8-15a, 18
Mark 1: 1-18

"In the beginning" is not a bad way to begin. The phrase immediately captures our attention, creating the desire to know what will come next. "In the beginning" is such a good way to begin that we tend to forget how much our everyday lives depend on the presumption that there was a beginning. Without "In the beginning," there would be no stories, no novels, no tall tales. Without "In the beginning," we could not make sense of our lives. "I was born in Dallas, Texas, on the twenty-fourth day of July in 1940." That we are able to say such sentences to one another is nothing short of a miracle. Just think how much you have learned from that sentence, eliciting as it does shared stories—for instance, "Texas," "1940," "born." No doubt, my story of Texas may not be the same story you entertain about Texas, but at least our different accounts of Texas make possible a conversation of discovery.

"In the beginning" reminds us that we are timeful creatures. We were not only created in time, but our very creation constitutes time. Perhaps no time of the church year better reminds us that we are creatures "caught in time" than Advent. At this time, we are reminded that there is another beginning than the beginning "in the beginning." The book of Mark

---

[10] I have borrowed this title from Nigel Biggar's book on Karl Barth's ethics, *The Hastening That Waits: Karl Barth's Ethics* (Oxford: Oxford University Press, 1993).

begins: "The beginning of the good news of Jesus Christ." The story, "In the beginning," is given a new dispensation that requires a new telling. Indeed, we believe the beginning signaled at the beginning of the book of Mark makes it possible for us to understand the significance of the first "In the beginning." Nicholas Lash reminds us:

> The spring festival, rather than mid-winter, once marked New Year's Day. On 25 March, according to the fifth-century calendar known as the martyrdom of Jerome, "Our Lord Jesus Christ was crucified, and conceived, and the world was made." On this day God brings all things alive, *ex nihilo*. Out of nothing, by his word, he makes a world, a home. Out of the virgin's womb, Christ is conceived. Out of that world threatening death on Calvary, life is new-born from an empty tomb. Christ's terror is God's Word's human vulnerability. But, it is just this vulnerability, this surrender, absolute relationship, which draws out of darkness finished life, forgiveness of sin.[11]

How extraordinary. God—the same God who creates all that is and will be—assumes the garment of our flesh. In time, God becomes subject to time making it possible for us patiently to live in time. We know this to be the case, affirming, as we do Eucharist after Eucharist, that God shows up in the bread and wine made by the Holy Spirit the body and blood of Christ. We know this, but we confess that we have a hard time living out these timeful and time constituting realities. God's gift of time is just that, a gift, and it must be received as gift. But such receiving threatens, forcing, as it does, the recognition that we are death destined creatures.

That we have a beginning is surely goods news, but a beginning implies an end. We fear that the name of that end is death, which does not sound like good news. Indeed, we fear that the prophecy in Isaiah is far too close to being the truth:

> All flesh is grass,
>   and all the goodliness thereof is

---

[11]Nicholas Lash, *Believing Three Ways in One God: A Reading of the Apostles' Creed* (Notre Dame: University of Notre Dame Press, 1992), 118.

> as the flower of the field:
> the grass withers, the flower fades;
> > because the spirit of the Lord blows upon it;
> > surely the people is grass.
> The grass withers, the flower fades:
> but the word of Our God shall stand for ever.

We wither like the grass. We fade like the flower. The gift of time is the gift of death—a death we fear renders meaningless all that we may be between our beginning and our end.

Because we find it difficult to imagine our beginning and ending determined by God's beginning and ending, the meaninglessness of our death-shadowed lives haunts modern consciousness. We desperately seek some means to know where we are in time. Constituted by time, we seek to flee time, to find a time outside time in the hope that we are something more than withered grass. Unwilling to be timed by God's time, we become lost in the cosmos. For example, consider this extraordinary hymn to nothingness written by William James in *The Varieties of Religious Experience*:

> Though the scientist may individually nourish a religion and be a theist in his irresponsible hours, the days are over when it could be said that for Science herself the heavens declare the glory of God and the firmament showeth his handiwork. Our solar system, with its harmonies, is seen now as but one passing case of a certain sort of moving equilibrium in the heavens, realized by a local accident in an appalling wilderness of worlds where no life can exist. In a span of time which as a cosmic interval will count but as an hour, it will have ceased to be. The Darwinian notion of chance production, and subsequent destruction, speedy or deferred, applies to the largest as well as the smallest facts. It is impossible, in the present temper of the scientific imagination, to find in the drifting of the cosmic atoms, whether they work on the universal or on the particular scale, anything but a kind of aimless weather, doing and undoing, achieving no proper history, and leaving no result. Nature has no one distinguishable ultimate

tendency with which it is possible to feel a sympathy. In the vast rhythm of her processes, as the scientific mind now follows them, she appears to cancel herself. The books of natural theology which satisfied the intellects of our grandfathers seem to us quite grotesque, representing, as they did, a God who conformed the largest things of nature to the paltriest of our private wants. The God whom science recognizes must be a God of universal laws exclusively, a God who does a wholesale, not a retail business. He cannot accommodate his processes to the convenience of individuals. The bubbles on the foam which coats a stormy sea are floating episodes, made and unmade by the forces of the wind and water. Our private selves are like those bubbles—epiphenomena, as Clifford, I believe, ingeniously called them; their destinies weigh nothing and determine nothing in the world's irremediable currents of events.[12]

James's characterization of the "scientific mind" now well describes our "minds." No matter how sincerely we may try to believe that "In the beginning, God," we know our lives are shaped by the knowledges and practices of a world no longer determined by God's time. We know our lives are like grass. But, such knowledge is not that determined by the God who speaks through the prophets. Rather, it is shaped by what I can only call the everyday nihilism that grips our lives—a nihilism that desperately strives against the meaninglessness we fear our deaths name to do something or be something that will not be erased by time.

So, we rage against time, not content to be creatures of God's time. We hope against hope, struggling to secure our existence against the outrageous fortune that we are accidents of time destined to disappear in time. In the meantime, we seek identifications that will assure we made some difference. For example, we take comfort that we are citizens of the reigning superpower of the world or, as some even presume, the greatest nation that has ever existed. Surely, to be part of such a people means we can secure ourselves against time. The very fact that national holidays are now more determinative for our lives than church time is but an indication that our lives are

---

[12]William James, *The Varieties of Religious Experience: A Study in Human Nature* (New York: Mentor Book, 1958), 406-408.

constituted by a story that begins "In the beginning, we have no choice but to create ourselves." We know the story that we can story our own lives to be a lie, but we are no less determined to live as if such a story is true. So, we live desperate lives in the vain hope that we can make the lie the truth through effort, which so often takes the form of love.

The result, of course, makes us the most impatient of people. We refuse to accept limits. There is no reason cancer cannot be cured. There is no reason that we should grow old. After all, is not aging but another illness to be conquered by medical science? Time is not a gift, but a scarce resource to be used efficiently. We have no time to take the time to care for this hungry person when so many are starving. Why take the time to feed one rather than work to overcome world hunger? Grandiosity is but the other side of a people made mad by the denial that we are time's creatures.

So, let us take comfort in this Advent. A time when we are reminded that time is not our time, but rather, that through our Baptism, we have been made participants in God's time. A time we fortunately do not know how to calculate. We do not know how to measure God's time because, as we are told in 2 Peter, the Lord's time is but the expression of God's patience. We quite literally cannot imagine God's time, but fortunately it has not been left up to our imaginations. Rather, we have been taught how to wait in time by the one who is God's patience. He, who could have commanded the Father's legions to save him, submitted to the cross making it possible for us to live lives of patience.

Christians live between times, but we have no way to know when the end comes or what it means for the "heavens to pass away." The good news is that we do not have to know in order to live hopeful and patient lives. Because it is God's time, the question for us, as is made clear in 2 Peter, is "what sort of persons ought you to be in leading lives of holiness and godliness?" Christ has died; Christ has risen; Christ will come again. Dying, rising, and coming again makes it possible for us to be a people who refuse to live desperate lives of impatience. God's hastening of the end is sure through Jesus, but Jesus's cross is a hastening that waits—a waiting designed to draw all of God's creation to the great consummation "where righteousness is at home."

So, come to this meal of the end time—a time that makes possible our living as creatures who know, "In the beginning, God...."

Disrupting Time

I confess, dear God, that the most difficult problem I have when I pray is how to begin. What do we do when we call on "God?" You have graciously given us your name, but "I am who I am" is, if you don't mind me saying so, vague. That name, if it is a name, invited us to address you by piling one big adjective on top of another big adjective—Most Holy, Most Gracious, Awesome, Omnipotent. Those adjectives give us the impression, when everything is said and done, that you are the "biggest thing around." But the biggest thing around will not fit in a manger. So, I pray, we pray, that you will send your Spirit to us to give us fresh tongues, so that when we pray, we will not be praying to our idea of you, but to you. How odd is it that you have made us praying animals through your gift of prayer. So, thank you, gracious Lord, for receiving our stuttering prayers. Transform them and us into your prayer for the world.

God, most days I think the hardest thing to have to do is pray. I can never decide how to begin—"Dear God," "Lord," "Father of our Lord Jesus Christ," "Holy One of Israel"—Jesus, all that seems like the same-old same-old. You have graciously given us your name, but I am not sure, and I expect most of us are not sure, what to do with it. I suspect that is my problem. I want a boring God, but when I get what I want I lose the ability to pray. So, come again, Father of our Lord Jesus Christ, frighten me so that I will remember what a wonderful thing, what a miraculous thing, you have done to give us the gift of prayer. Give us your Spirit that we may learn to pray as one.

Disrupting Time

Unrelenting, You will not let us alone. Do you have to be so insistent? We think we would like you to be faithful, but your faithfulness can become a bit tiresome. Surely, you must need a rest from your pursuit of us? For example, did you really need Israel all that much? You just would and will not leave her alone. We think of poor Jonah, poor Job, and poor Jeremiah—God, what your faithfulness put them through. Just as you refuse to abandon Israel, so you refuse to abandon us, your confused and confusing people called church. You called us into being by that great faithfulness called Jesus. Did you really have to take on our condition in order to speak, to get in our faces? Of course, such questions make no sense because, whether we like it or not, you have done and do what you have done. Can we dare to ask you to make us faithful witnesses to your fidelity? We suspect that if we became even a little faithful the world would dislike us in a matter not unlike our dislike for your faithfulness. What a bind you put us in. We pray, however, that we may learn, Mary-like, to say, "Here I am," fearing no longer your faithfulness, but rejoicing that you have given us lives worth living.

Aldersgate Sermons

"What is truth?" is Pilate's question, our question, Lord of all that is. An innocent question, a good question, we think. We ask, "What is truth?" hoping to delay indefinitely any claim that threatens our souls. Taking the way of the skeptic, the cynic, we think, is the way to serve you as the only truth. So you alone are truth, which means that we have, like Pilate, no means to grasp the truth that shows up on our doormat dressed in dirt. Quite frankly, God, we prefer our truth to come in more mundane forms—sayings like, "Well, I guess when it is all said and done we each have to make up our own minds." What shit, but how we do love our comforts. So, all we ask is to use this prayer to discomfort our presumption that truth is to be found in us. Frighten us into the recognition that the truth is the cross of Jesus that puts us at cross-purposes with the world. Help us learn the difference, however, between being the difference your truth makes and just being different. Make us your beautiful, truthful people.

Disrupting Time

Devious, dear God, are we devious. We believe we can hide from you. We even believe we can hide from ourselves. "I'm not really who you think I am" is a play we play on a daily basis. For better or worse, and usually it is for the worse, we even end up becoming what we pretend to be. As a result, we begin to hate ourselves, our neighbors, and You. In particular, we hate because you refuse to believe that we are who we pretend to be. Help us learn to trust your love. Help us to learn we do not need to pretend to hide from your perfect love. Help us accept the joy that comes from the honesty your love makes possible. Forgiven, by God, you have forgiven the pretense that nailed your Son to the cross. Forgiven, you have given us a way to go on in a lie-shaped world. As your forgiven people, make us your salvation, that the world may see how wonderful it is to be no more or less than we are, that is, your creatures.

Like Those Who Dream

Psalm 128
Luke 3:1-6

I always loved Mrs. Peters' Sunday School Class. She enthralled our five-year imaginations with her unparalleled flannel-board talks. Indeed, that is the way I learned most of the early stories of the Bible. If you could not make the story fit on the flannel-board, you could live without it.

For example, I have never forgotten Mrs. Peters' rendering of the sacrifice of Isaac. I remember the large green felt, Abraham, Isaac and the donkeys in the lower left-hand corner, the mountain in Moriah in the upper right-hand corner. Mrs. Peters told us that God had told Abraham that he must sacrifice Isaac. She knew that this might disturb some five year olds who were beginning to feel the threat of their fathers. So, rather than keeping us in suspense she quickly took out a large wooly ram and placed it on the mountain, saying, "Don't worry, God is going to supply a ram so Isaac won't have to be killed."

I was in seminary before I realized, through reading Kierkegaard's *Fear and Trembling*, that God did not tell Abraham or Isaac that there was going to be a ram in the bush. Abraham had to walk all the way up that mountain thinking, "This is it. I am going to have to kill Isaac." God was not playing, and there was no assurance that things were going to come out all right.

I tell this story because I think when we enter the season of Advent it is as if we Christians say to ourselves, "Let us play like we need to wait for awhile. Let us play like we need to be those to whom John preached who had to repent." In short, "Let us play like we are Jews."

This playing at Advent, of course, invites the most invidious of contrasts between Christians and Jews: Jews, we think, do not know fulfillment because they do not believe the Messiah has come. They are, therefore, a people permanently on hold. They have plenty of hope and some patience, but their task is to wait. In contrast, we Christians are people of fulfillment because we know the Messiah has come. We do not need to wait. We have been given the truth, so our task is to simply get on with it. We remind ourselves once a year that we ought to play as if we have to wait, but in truth, that is not our game.

In this respect, of course, the practice of receiving gifts at Christmas becomes our paradigmatic experience for "waiting," for we cannot help but think of Advent like wanting to get a bicycle for Christmas. When we were between the ages of six and ten we were pretty sure we were going to get a bicycle, but we subjected ourselves to doubt about whether we were really going to get a bicycle (or a puppy) because we wanted to be surprised. After all, surprises are half the fun. In like manner, we Christians play at being Jews for a month so we can be surprised every year, but we know we are not "waiters."

The difficulty we Christians have with learning to wait has spawned the well-known genre of Advent sermon. Since we Christians really do not believe that we are a people who have to learn to wait, we turn waiting, and correlatively, hoping, into general anthropological characteristics intrinsic to the human condition. So we say things like: "Without hope we die." "Without dreams life is meaningless." So Advent is that time of hopeful waiting in which we are reminded that life is always about living suspended between our hopes and their fulfillments.

There can be profound ways of displaying this, such as William Lynch's extraordinary reflections in *Image of Hope* on the relationship between the absence of hope and mental illness. American capitalism gives us another account of the relationship between hope and fulfillment by suggesting that if we just learn to be patient and work hard our hopes will be rewarded. Thus, we believe, if we just keep working hard we may eventually graduate from the Divinity School, get a Ph.D., or become a full professor. I often think that about the cruelest thing that can ever happen to anyone is to have his or her profoundest desires fulfilled.

The problem with these general anthropological characterizations about the relationship between waiting and hope is that they have nothing to do with Jesus. Indeed, they have nothing to do with the Jews. Hope for Christians and Jews is hope in a very specific, fleshy, material fulfillment that requires an equally specific form of waiting. Those who gave us Psalm 126 wanted Zion restored. Zion restored is a dream to be realized, a dream formed by the materiality of that fortress city. Then and then alone would the nations see that "the Lord has done great things for them." This hope is as concrete as the restoration of the watercourses of the Negeb. They wanted real water to drink.

We Christians, of course, have tended to spiritualize our hopes because we fear Jewish hopes. After all, Jesus is the Messiah of the Jews, and we are not quite prepared for Jewish rejection of our Messiah. Jews note, after all, that they also hope in a Messiah, but a Messiah capable of restoring Zion.

For example, it was a Jewish hope that Jesus read in the synagogue: "He has anointed me to preach good news to the poor. He has sent me to proclaim release to the captives and recovery of sight to the blind, to set at liberty those who are pressed, to proclaim the acceptable year of Yahweh" (Luke 4:18-19, Isaiah 61:1-2). But the Jews ask: "What happened? That does not sound like the world we live in." Like John sending his disciples to Jesus, they ask, "Are you the one who is to come, or are we to wait for another?" Jesus answered them, "Go and tell John what you have seen and heard: the blind received their sight, the lame walk, the lepers are cleansed, the deaf hear, the dead are raised, the poor have good news brought to them. And blessed is anyone who takes no offense at me" (Matt. 11:3-6).

The Jews ask what happened. If this Messiah is the Messiah of the golden age, we still seem to live in a world of war, of blindness, of the lame, the oppressed and the down trodden. Where is the golden age we were promised as the Messianic age? Surely, this cannot be the Messiah.

There is no easy way to avoid these questions. Indeed, I have always been fond of the Apostate Julian's attempt to defeat Christianity. Julian hated Jews only a little less than he hated Christians. However, as a committed pagan, he had not suffered directly at the hands of Jewish tutors the way he had at those of Christian teachers. Accordingly, he called the Jews to him and gave them money to rebuild the temple in Jerusalem, because Christians made so much of the fact that the temple had been destroyed and not rebuilt. Julian clearly understood the heart of the matter, because he knew better than to separate issues of truth from the issues of Zion. He had learned much from his Christian tutors, after all.

He thus reasoned that if the temple were rebuilt it would show that Christians were at a disadvantage when compared to Jews. Christians subsequently made much of the fact that soon after the rebuilding began an earthquake struck Jerusalem destroying the beginnings of the new temple. Julian, moreover, was killed in short order.

We are embarrassed by such polemics. We want to say that truth is spiritual. Yet, Christians no less than Jews were and are people whose hopes are material. That is why we cannot play at waiting. Jesus is no Messiah who promises that if we just learn to wait our hopes will be fulfilled. Rather, Jesus is our Jewish temple who has made us, Gentiles, part of God's promise to be God's own material presence in the world, that the world might know what kind of God governs the sun, stars, and our lives.

As Christians, we badly distort our faith when we think that our Messiah has made us other than the Jews. Rather, the salvation that has been wrought in Christ has established a new time when even we Gentiles can become part of God's promising people, who rightly witness to the world that our lives, after Jesus, are eschatologically determined. For it is the world's presumption that our existence has an outcome that we can guarantee through our hopes. It is the Jew and the Christian who stand in the world, reminding the world that our outcome is not in our own hands but in God's.

In my course in Christian Ethics I often suggest that Christians are not called to nonviolence because we believe nonviolence promises to rid the world of war; but, in a world of war we cannot imagine being anything other than nonviolent as faithful followers of Christ. Christians can wait nonviolently in a world at war because we know the materiality of our God in the person of Jesus of Nazareth. We, therefore, do not hold out any vain hope in the general notion of peace separate from the peace that is embodied in this man Jesus. That is a hard and painful waiting in a world of so much injustice, but we Christians must so wait, not because the Kingdom did not come, but because it did, taking the form of this man—God—who would not have the Kingdom violently realized.

Therefore, if we play at waiting during Advent we will destroy ourselves and fail to be witnesses to the God who calls us to be the eschatological people of the new age. We will be like those who submerge Christ's cross in the resurrection, as if Christ went to his death knowing he would be raised. That makes the gospel a dumb show and our lives a dumb show, as if we are only playing at death and life. Christ's death is as real as the land of Palestine. If his death is not at least that real then his resurrection is equally an illusion.

That is why this fleshy meal of Christ's body and blood is absolutely crucial for us to learn what it means to be a people trained to wait and hope. For here, time and time again, we feed on God's bodily presence so that we might rightly learn to hope and wait. For this meal is Kingdom come, it is our waiting feast, through which the world is given hope by being made part of God's dream. So, come celebrating here our inclusion as "people of the dream," who rightly have learned what a joy it is to have been engrafted into God's promise, called Israel.

Disrupting Time

Endless complexity threatens to make living impossible. So we would like you, dear Father, to be simple. You are, of course, simple. Only you can be what you do. Only you can be fully yourself and fully in your Son and Spirit. But that you can be what you do threatens us even more than the complexity of our confused lives. So we take refuge in our complexities, comforting ourselves with the illusion that no one, not even you, can understand us. You tell us, "Do not murder, steal, and lie," but surely, learning to worship you has to be more complex, more difficult than such simple imperatives. Yet your word is plain as the book of James: "You want something and do not have it; so you commit murder." Surely, it can't be that simple. But it is simple. So we pray that you will continue to call us from our "complexities," that we may learn to enjoy the beauty of your simplicity.

Aldersgate Sermons

Wordy Lord, you have graced us with your Word, your Son, so that we might be people capable of speaking truthfully to one another. Through your Word, you have taught us words matter. We must learn the discipline of your speech, but we swim in a sea of words, tempting us to think one word is as good as another word. It is as if we can go on holiday from the exacting task of speaking, of praying, of and to you. So send us poets pledged to word care, that we might learn why only this word will do. Make us eloquent embodiments of your Word. Make us glad proclaimers of your Word, reveling in the wonder that you would speak through us. Amen.

Disrupting Time

Timeful Lord, you sought us out through your Son, through water and Spirit baptized, rescuing us from false eternities, that we might be your timeful people. As we come to the end of this course, help us remember that in you all endings are but beginnings. We pray that you make more of this time than we can imagine. As your people we know you make our past more than we knew and fill our future with the unexpected—thus making our present joy. As a people caught up in that joy, may our study be an alternative to the world's despair. We praise you for giving us the time and space amidst the pain and injustice of this world to read books. May our study, may our reading, may our prayers be peace so that the world might know that through your Son's cross and resurrection your truth is deeper than our violence.

Infinite, I wonder what I mean when I address you as "infinite." Do I know what it means to be finite? If I do not have a hold on finite, then what can I mean when I call you and address you as infinite? Big words seem necessary for our idea of you. But then, you refuse to be our idea, even a big idea. Instead, you show up in a Virgin's belly. So let us begin again. Maybe "infinite" reminds us that your love cannot be used up. For us existence seems like a zero sum game. "I just have so much to give," we say. The notion that the more we give the more we have to give is foreign to us. Yet, we believe you have made us participants in the gift of your Son—a gift that cannot be used up. So let us rejoice when a stranger claims us as friend. Through such friendship, we are expanded into more than we could even imagine. The life you give us is weird and wonderful. Thank God, it is so, as otherwise we would die of boredom.

Disrupting Time

Lord of the waters, you have set us adrift on a trackless ocean, in a leaky boat, with no oars or rudder. "Rudderless" nicely describes our situation, but matters are worse. Even if we had a rudder, we would not know which direction to go. We are not even sure if there are any directions—or, if there are directions, we so distrust our wants that we do not know which way we really want to go. In short, we feel lost and, so feeling, think it is probably your fault. Yet, you refuse to let us drown in self-pity and blame. Instead, you drown us in your good kingdom, that death and resurrection of Jesus our Lord, making us part of that great ark, your church. The winds of your love blow that ark out to sea, away from the shores we think might provide safety, so that we might take on board the drowning. How wonderful it is that the more we are taken on board, the less your ark is crowded and the safer we are. Thank you for making us steady sailors who have no reason to fear the unknown, having learned you would have us be at sea. Amen.

Jews and the Eucharist

Genesis 28:10-22
Romans 8:12-25
Matthew 13:24-30, 36-43

We are not a church that often celebrates the Eucharist. I regret that and would like us to move toward celebrating every Sunday. There are many reasons Protestant churches do not regularly celebrate Eucharist, but I think that the main reason is most of us no longer believe our salvation comes through the Jews. I realize this claim will strike many as fantastic, but by the time I finish, I hope it will at least make sense—as well as create in us a hunger to feast with our God.

The text we heard from Romans is, of course, part of the problem. The text itself is not the problem, but how we hear it is. We are told not to live according to the flesh, "for if you live according to the flesh, you will die; but if by the Spirit you put to death the deeds of the body, you will live." Our problem is that such a text reinforces our presumption that Christianity is about the "spiritual," and on the whole we like it like that. By spiritual, we usually mean it is about stuff too deep to understand, but nonetheless important.

We also think that the spiritual contrasts with all the things that make life good. To be spiritual is to be anti-body, anti-sex, anti-pleasure. So to be spiritual means to be good but dull. This really does not sound like terribly good news, but then if Christianity is really about the spiritual we are pretty much left alone to do what we want with the stuff that really matters, that is, the body, sex, and money.

We should not be surprised that we associate Christianity with this sense of the spiritual, especially given the world in which we live. If we did not put God in something like the "spiritual realm," we would not know where else God might be. We know that no matter how much our belief in God might matter to us—and I know that it matters a great deal to most of you—most of us live our lives as practical atheists. We think we need God to give "meaning" to our lives, but if in fact it turns out that God just is not God, most of us would not have to change how we live. We could go on doing pretty much what we are doing.

For example, Paul tells us, "The creation waits with eager longing for the revealing of the children of God . . . . We know that the whole creation has been groaning in labor pains until now; and not only the creation, but we ourselves, who have the first fruits of the Spirit, groan inwardly while we wait for adoption, the redemption of our bodies." Think about how that set of claims would play in any public school in America. All creation—rocks, plains, mountains, trees, cats, dogs, moles, weeds, and even we are longing, Paul says, for the revealing of the children of God.

We may think that this is a colorful way to see the world, but we do not have the slightest idea what difference such a view might make for the way we conduct our science or our everyday life. We need our nature dead, subject to the laws of cause and effect, so we can subject it to our purposes—purposes, of course, that are meant to serve human well being. We do not believe that what we call nature is best understood as creation. In this sense, the creationists are right to suggest that the way children are taught to view "nature" in the public schools makes any claim that we and the world are God's good creation irrelevant. I know that we would like to believe that we and the universe exist as gift, as God's good creation, but it is hard to know what creation means once we have learned to view the world "scientifically."

So Christianity becomes that name for a set of beliefs we cannot "prove"—that is why we call it "faith." Faith is a kind of "knowledge," but it is personal. It means a lot to me, but I cannot presume that anyone else ought to share it. Most people who come to church probably believe some of the same stuff, but I cannot say that anyone who does not believe it is any the worse for it.

The story of Jacob's dream stands in stark contrast with this understanding of "faith." One of the worst sermons I ever heard was on this passage. The preacher tried to make Jacob meet our understanding of Christianity as spiritual, as a meaningful experience. He noted that Jacob was on the whole a pretty unsavory character—a kid spoiled by his mother, a thief who stole his brother's birthright, a schemer who deserved to have Laban as a father-in-law—but this preacher said that Jacob had this wonderful dream that changed his life. Such dreams, he assured us, were the way ancient people described important religious experiences. Moreover, we know Jacob had been changed by this wonderful experience because the first thing he did on awaking was to pray.

The only problem with this way of telling this story is that it fails to attend to the content of the prayer. Jacob was not in the least changed by his dream. All that the dream taught him was that God is present in this place in a peculiar manner, but he was not a bit intimidated by that knowledge. He was the same old Jacob, so he set out to strike a bargain with God: "If you will give me what I want, take care of my food and clothing, then you will be my God and I will even erect a house for you and give a tenth of what you give me." This is a man who knows how to strike a deal.

As moderns, we try to naturalize such passages by giving them a spiritual meaning. By doing so, however, we miss that Jacob, unsavory though he is, recognizes that God is at Bethel in a way that God is not everywhere. This place is different because this God is not some generalized spirit we need to give meaning to our lives. No, this is the God of Abraham and Isaac. This is the God of this land, the land of Palestine, which is given to Jacob, who is going to need it because he is going to have many descendants.

Moreover, the people of this land, Jacob's descendants, are God's people in a way no others are God's people. All the families of the earth will be blessed through these people, but they are different from such families, for God says, you—that is, the Jews—I have chosen to be my people, a people spread throughout the world. Though scattered abroad, I will also bring you back to this land, Palestine, because I keep my promises. You may learn to like Babylonia, Spain, or America, but as a people, you belong in Palestine. One can well understand why, after all the Jews have gone through since the time of Jacob, they are sometimes tempted to think, "Is this a promise we want?"

Let us confess that the Jacob story bothers us. God present in the land of Palestine in a different way than God is anywhere else just seems wrong. Is God not everywhere? Yes, but God's presence everywhere does not mean that God is not present in Palestine in a way that is different.

Surely, it is an arrogant and elitist claim to suggest that God is the God of the Jews in a different way than God is a God for everyone. It may sound arrogant to those of us who like to think God is the great democratic politician running the bureaucracies fairly, but I tell you this, if God is not the God of the Jews then our faith is in vain. Put as starkly as I can put it: if Christian envy of the Jews is ever so effective that we are able to destroy the last Jew from the face of the earth, then God will destroy the earth. Our God is not some generalized spirit, but a fleshy God whose body is the Jews.

That God, the God of the Jews, is the God we Christians believe has come in Jesus of Nazareth. We should not be surprised that the God of Abraham, Isaac, and Jacob would so come because God has no fear of the material—after all, it is God's own creation waiting in eager longing. God came in this man, Jesus, to engraft us Gentiles into the promise to Israel. God is present in Jesus in a way God is present nowhere else. Through that presence, we have been made part of Israel's blessing so that we too might be a blessing to the nations. God does not save us, Jew, Christian, and everyone else, by giving us a better set of philosophical ideas about how to live; God saves us through setting up this rock in Palestine called Jesus. Through Jesus' life, death, and resurrection, we have been made part of God's life with the Jews. All creation rejoices in our creation as God's people, for we are what God has always desired as the end of creation.

That God's salvation is so fleshly, so material, is why we are here to worship God in one another's presence. We know we cannot hear the word as isolated spirits, but rather we hear God's word as God's body. Through the hearing of the word, God creates a unity unknown anywhere else. Of course, that is why nothing could be more scandalous than for Christians to kill one another. When we do so, we commit suicide.

The unity God creates by making us the body of Christ is most vividly present in Eucharist. Through that bread and wine, which is the body and blood of Christ, we become God's body. Such presence is made known because our savior is no dead hero, but the resurrected Lord. Resurrection does not mean that Jesus, after laying a few insights and ideals on us, took a flier, leaving us alone to deal with this mess. Resurrection means that when the words are said—"This is my body. . . . This is my blood. . . . Pour out your Holy Spirit on these gifts"—there is nothing we can do to prevent God from being present.

It is frightening, is it not? As Jacob says, "Surely the Lord is in the place—and I did not know it," and then we are told, "And he was afraid." I do not blame him in the slightest. God *is* frightening. Indeed, I sometimes think the reason that Protestants, and in particular Methodists, are more likely to believe in the "real absence" than the "real presence" is that God just scares the hell out of us—and for good reason if God just is this God of Abraham, Isaac, Jacob, and Jesus.

Yet, God's unrelenting refusal to be "spiritualized" is particularly threatening in the light of our Gospel for this morning. The parable of the wheat and the tares has been used, particularly in recent times, to challenge the Christian presumption that we are better than other people or know something others do not. Thus, we are told that in this time between the times we really do not know who has been bad or good until next Christmas. We are comforted by the suggestion that "until the end of the age" we really cannot tell who are the children of the kingdom and who are the children of the evil one. So, who are we to judge—particularly ourselves? We are all equally sinners, which is good news because I am freed from thinking that how I live matters to God.

But, once this parable is read eucharistically we see that it is no accident that the kingdom of heaven is like a good field of wheat. Wheat becomes bread, and through the Spirit, bread becomes the body and blood of Christ. God is present here in this meal in a way God is present nowhere else. We are that wheat; we are that bread, which the families of the world need if they are to know God. We are the people on which the peace of God depends. We are God's eucharist; we are those children for which creation had been longing. In the celebration of this meal, God lifts us up as he lifted Christ on the cross, so that the world might see the beauty of God's creation made real in a people at peace with their world. How can we not hunger to share this meal and share it often? May God continue to make us hungry for it. Amen and Amen!

Disrupting Time

Dear God, how we Christians fear the Jews. Unpleasant people, argumentative people—do they not know you want us to be nice? We are also aware that they were your people before we were your people. How we are both your people we do not understand. So, we ask that you may give us, Jew and Christian, the patience to rest easy in the knowledge that you have bound us in a common destiny. May the world look to us as exemplifications of how an argument across time gives us time to learn to love one another. Yom Kippur—the day of repentance, a holy day—is such a time. Help us Christians, to repent of our disdain for Jewish repentance and, so repented, join in the eternal embrace called your kingdom.

Aldersgate Sermons

A New Year, Master of the universe, a day of repentance for your promised people. A dangerous year, I fear, due to our fear, Christian fear of those who say they are Israel's enemies. American Christians are frightened, not because we are Christian, but because we are American. We American Christians are tempted to seek safety by forgetting yet again the Jews. But you have taught us, time and time again, often through the judgment of Jewish suffering, that when we forget the Jews, we become less your church. The way forward is clouded for us, for Jews, for Muslims. Teach us how to go on as your timeful peoples, seeking no escape from time. May Christ, your fiery cloud of repentance, guide us on the way, saving us from too easy reconciliation and sentimental embraces. Help us see that the way forward begins in the confession of our sin.

Master of the Universe, through your son you would have us be your friend. But what could it possibly mean for us to be friends of God? Friendship with other people is hard enough. To be your friend is quite simply unimaginable. Friendship with you is right up there with asking us to be friends with our worst enemy, but then, maybe you are our worst enemy. Maybe I am my worst enemy. So, if you are nearer to us than we are to ourselves, unless we become friends with you we cannot become friends with ourselves or anyone else. This business of friendship must take time, but thank God your patience with us gives us all the time we need. Make us your friends so that when the puzzled world cannot figure out what makes us Christians the same, they will say, "But see how they love one another."

God and the Fourth of July

Psalms 45: 10-17
Genesis 24: 34-38, 42-49, 58-67
Romans 7: 15-25
Matthew 11: 16-19, 25-30

Our pastor may well have put her soul in jeopardy by asking me to preach today, that is, on the Fourth of July. By that, I do not mean that some of you may get so upset by what I have to say, that you will blame Susan for asking me to preach. Unfortunately, I suspect that I am no longer able to get that kind of reaction at Aldersgate because over the years you have come to know me and what I think. Therefore, no matter what I might say, you think, "Oh! That's just Stanley." I have to say that I am not entirely happy with that reaction, because when I preach I assume that I am not giving you my views, but rather proclaiming God's word—a word that is meant to enliven us and, in so doing, offer promise for the world.

That turns out to be the reason asking me to preach today puts Susan's soul in jeopardy, for such an invitation creates what the Catholics call a "near occasion of sin." By that, they mean that if you have brothers or sisters in Christ whom you know have certain weaknesses, it is a sin to create an opportunity that will tempt them to do what they are tempted to do. Susan knows the Fourth of July is not exactly my best time. To ask me to preach on the Fourth tempts me to do what I said no preacher should do, namely, use the sermon to impose on you my opinions rather than proclaim the Gospel. The problem is not just my opinions, all of which—I have to say—are true, but my anger.

I want to be clear that there is nothing wrong with anger. Our Lord was obviously—as we say down home—"none too pleased" with the generation he confronted. That generation was incapable of being pleased: John fasted and was condemned, Jesus ate and drank and was condemned. You just cannot please some people. However, anger can be a problem when that which we ought to love does not school it. I fear that my reaction to the Fourth may boil over to no good result. I might say something like, "Our understanding of church-state relations in America 'impoverishes most of our discussions of religion and politics. National feasts and ceremonies replaced the liturgical calendar of the church, whose feasts become private observances. . . . National holidays have become primarily occasions for private recreation.'" I might say something like that, but I do not have to because Archbishop Cardinal George of Chicago just said it.

My reaction to the Fourth is much less sophisticated. For example, in 1992 something called the C.S. Lewis Foundation asked me to give a paper at their annual meeting in Oxford. Paula and I thought this would give us an opportunity to go back to Ireland as well as see Wales before turning up at the conference, so I accepted. I need to be clear—and I realize some of you may be great C.S. Lewis fans—I like Lewis well enough, but I usually cannot stand to be around admirers of C.S. Lewis. I particularly cannot stand American admirers who are so taken with Lewis that they go to a conference in England so they can be close to where he lived. In the enthusiasm for returning to places Paula and I so enjoy, I conveniently allowed myself to forget that I would not be in, so to speak, my natural environment.

As soon as we drove into Oxford and settled in at the conference, I realized I had made a big mistake. I just did not share much with these folk. However, since I am a Protestant and from the lower classes, I always try to do my duty. So, I dutifully showed up at 8:00 of the morning on which I was to give my talk at 8:30. It was in a church that, as the British put it, had become "redundant" and was now used as an auditorium. I sat down sleepily, having little sense where I was. Indeed, as is often the case when you are traveling, I had no idea what day it was. I soon discovered, however, that it was the Fourth of July, when the from-my-point-of-view-far-too-enthusiastic person charged with warming up the audience said, "We all know what day it is; let's show the Brits what we are made of." He then had all the Americans stand and sing the National Anthem.

I was aghast. The Iraqi war had just ended, if it has ever ended, in which we, that is, we Americans, began to believe that you could have a war in which no one, or at least no American, gets killed. I was introduced, and before I knew it, I said something like this: "How can you do that? I understand you are in England, and it seems like fun to thumb your nose at the British, but you are not Americans; you are Christians. You are part of a nation that has just slaughtered thousands in a desert. Even on just war grounds, this is not a time for celebration but for mourning. So, please, never do that again." Paula arrived just as I finished my diatribe and was beginning my lecture. She can testify that I had managed to create in my audience a hostility that was quite remarkable even among people who thought that if C.S. Lewis had not existed they could not believe in Jesus.

I have told you this story to help you understand why Susan's soul is in jeopardy for placing this temptation in my path, that is, for giving me the opportunity to rake us over the coals for the general American penchant for confusing church and nation. After all, if you think what Archbishop Cardinal George says is true—which I certainly do—then you cannot deny that we manage fairly well at Aldersgate, at least in terms of our worship, with how we handle the national holidays: we ignore them. Susan always reminds us that the nation's time is not the church's time; so, for example, Thanksgiving can never be more important than Christmas, and for us Pentecost makes the Fourth of July a minor secular holiday. If we acknowledge secular holidays at all, we usually do so as part of our prayers of intercession. We rightly thank God on the Fourth of July that we live in a country in which we enjoy freedom from tyranny as well as material prosperity. Overall, I think that this is a very intelligent strategy; but I also fear that if we just ignore the Fourth, we might believe that the Fourth has no hold over our lives. Accordingly, we end up being more determined by the sentiments that the Fourth represents than we should be as Christians. Therefore, I am going to give in to the temptation Susan has placed before me and preach about how as Christians we can negotiate this celebration of nation.

Disrupting Time

Fortunately, King David's Psalm appointed for today is directly relevant for helping us understand how we, Christ's body, should navigate the waters that threaten to drown us in the flood unleashed by July Fourth. Psalm 45 is about the celebration of a royal wedding. The bride is told:

> Forget your own people and your father's house;
> and, when the king desires your beauty,
> remember that he is your lord.
> Do him obeisance, daughter of Tyre,
> and the richest in the land will court you with gifts.

Because we know that our king is Christ, this cannot help but be a wonderful description of and advice for us, Christ's church. Through Christ's death, we have been ransomed from the powers of this world and made beautiful. Attracted to such a Lord, we forget our own people as well as our father's house, because we have been made part of such an extraordinary new people. That is why we are given names when we are baptized. We are given names so that we may be called by our Lord when he desires our beauty.

Accordingly, like Rebecca, when asked if she would go with Abraham's servant, we can gladly say, "Yes, I will go." Now in truth, like Rebecca, we often have little idea where our Lord is asking us to go. Our people and our father's house can look very good indeed if we find ourselves, as Rebecca did, in the desert on the back of a camel wondering who that strange person was who was coming her way. We may begin by thinking that going to church is not such a big deal, but before you know it we are in Lithuania. Even more mysterious, we discover that we are glad we are in Lithuania. There is nothing we would rather do than be in Lithuania because it makes us so happy.[13]

After all, as the Psalm makes clear, this is entirely about desire. The

---

[13] One of the members of Aldersgate, Grace Hachney, had gone to Lithuania because her husband, Tony Hachney, had a Fulbright there. She discovered a Methodist Church coming back to life after the 1989 rebirth. She became immersed in the church and led two work teams from our church to go to Lithuania to help the church there. I am happy to say that Grace discovered in the process that she was called to the ministry and is now, after completing Duke Divinity School, serving as a minister in North Carolina.

King desires the beauty of his queen, our Lord desires the beauty of his church, and we discover that our most passionate desire is to be desired by the one alone worthy of such desire. In our gospel, we are told that only the Son, who alone knows the Father and to whom all has been entrusted, has chosen to make his Father known to us. He has done so not because we are wise or learned, but because we are infants. You may not think that being called an infant is a compliment unless you remember that this is about desire. To be an infant, to be a child, is to be what we always are but often forget we are—a mass of desire. Moreover, as we grow more sophisticated, we learn to deny that even our sophistication is desire, which results in the corruption of our desires just to the extent that we think we can know and determine what we want.

Jesus says we will find his yoke good and his load light because in him we will rediscover our hearts' desires. I have to tell you, however, that I have always found that hard to believe. After all, Jesus ended up on a cross. Moreover, Christianity always seems to be about stuff that you do not want to do but which in the long run is probably a good idea to do. Yet, even if it works out OK in the long run, being a Christian still feels like being in a perpetual double bind. I suspect that many of us identify with what we take to be Paul's description of his life. He does not even do what he wants to do and often he hates that which he does. That, of course, is how the law works when it is not the law of Christ. Nothing makes us desire anything more than telling us we cannot have it. Most of the time we did not even know we wanted what was forbidden until it was forbidden.

Yet, the reason Jesus' yoke is good and his load is light is that, through what he gives us to do, his new law, we discover we desire to be our King's desired. To leave your people and your father's house is not work; rather, it is the discovery that we have relatives in Lithuania we did not know we had. Not only do we discover our heart's desire, but also others are attracted to us because we are so happy. Even more than being happy, we are made beautiful by the "unselfing" made possible by our Lord's gentleness and humility. So, we should not be surprised that the church moves through the ages sustained by the memory of the saints whose beauty shines across time.

This, of course, brings me back to the Fourth of July and to why, as

Christians, it is not exactly our day. It is not "not our day" because Christians must oppose nationalism, though we should. It is not "not our day" because America is an imperial power whose use of the military is increasingly indiscriminate and disproportionate, though as Christians committed to peace that is a development we must oppose. It is not "not our day" because the United States is somehow more immoral and evil than other nations, though as Christians we cannot help but be concerned with what John Paul II has called the "culture of death" that haunts our lives. The Fourth is not a problem for us because of what we are against; it is a problem because our desires have been formed by our Lord. We are simply so consumed by the consummation of Christ with his bride, the church, that we find celebrations like the Fourth of July distracting.

But, the bands and the fireworks are so undeniably entertaining. I am surely not suggesting we should avoid such entertainment. No, I will not tell you that. However, I will point out that if such entertainment seems more compelling than the celebration of this meal we are to share together then we have a problem. For in this Eucharist God gives to us the very body and blood of his Son so that our desires will become part of God's desire of his world. This is the end of all sacrifice, particularly the sacrifices made in the name of nations, so that we can rest in the presence of one another without fear, envy, and violence. In this meal, the beauty of our Lord blazes across the sky, rendering pale all other celebrations. So, come and taste the goodness and beauty of our God, and, in so consuming, may we be a people who may even be able to enjoy the Fourth without being consumed by it.

Prayer written thirty minutes after the destruction of the World Trade Center

Vulnerable—we feel vulnerable, God, and we are not used to feeling vulnerable. We are Americans.

Nor are we used to anyone hating us this much. Such terrible acts. Killing civilians. We are dumbfounded. Lost.

We are good people. We are a nation of peace. We do not seek war. We do not seek violence.

Try to help us remember that how we feel may be how the people of Iraq have felt while we have been bombing them. It is hard for us to acknowledge the "we" in "We bombed them."

What are we to do? We not only feel vulnerable, but we also feel helpless. We are not sure what to feel except shock, which will quickly turn to anger and even more suddenly to vengeance.

We are Christians. What are we to do as Christians? We know that anger will come to us. It does us no good for us to tell ourselves not to be angry. To try not to be angry just makes us all the more furious.

You, however, have given us something to do. We can pray, but we wonder for what we can pray. To pray for peace, to pray for the end of hate, to pray for the end of war seems platitudinous in this time.

Yet, of course, when we pray you make us your prayer to the world. So, Lord of peace, make us what you will. This may be one of the first times we have prayed that prayer with an inkling of how frightening prayer is. Help us.

Disrupting Time

September 11, 2001, we are told, forever changed our lives. What are we, the people of your cross, to make of such a claim? We are alleged to believe that Jesus' death on the cross forever changed all that exists, including us. In truth, September 11, 2001 seems more real than the hard wood of your Son's cross. That cross, your Son's cross, seems "back then," lost in the mists of history. The horror of September 11, 2001 dwarfs Christ's crucifixion. Yet, surely, if we are to comprehend the terror of September 11, 2001, if we are able to acknowledge such evil and still know how to go on, we will do so only by clinging to the Christ's cross. So, we pray that you will teach us to pray as cruciform people, capable of resisting the attraction and the beauty of the evil that September 11, 2001 names.

Furious, Spirit of Pentecost, I am furious. Suddenly, your creation, your church, looks so damned ugly. Where in the world are you in this mess? Christians in America suddenly celebrate the "we" of being Americans. God, it feels so good to have a "we," to be a community, to be united. We have been so lonely. Strangers discover that they are friends. But *that* we threatens to engulf the "we" bestowed at Pentecost. Reclaim us for yourself. Make the oneness of our link bestowed through baptism be a oneness so compelling that we are not tempted to be communities driven and created by fear. Make us truthful speakers of your Word. Make us speak the truth in love, seeking not to kill but to build. Make us a steadfast, patient, apocalyptic people, who know this is a long-haul kind of thing. Help us acknowledge that the kingdom come for which we pray is here in such patience. But, Jesus, Lord, it is hard to be your people.

Disrupting Time

Two years later, the fear remembered, the horror relived, will we ever be free of September 11, 2001. Lord of death, we confess that we cannot will our imaginations free of those terror-shaped images. Time may heal wounds, but these wounds continue to fester. Life must return to normal, but to what end? Time, the time created at Pentecost, seems so unreal to us. Yet, if that time is unreal what are we doing in this place set aside to study your Word? Is this how you, Lord of life, would have us resist the culture of death? We make no easy promises that we are going to do better, be better, your people. The best we can do is not to pretend that we know what you will have us say or be. May you use our lack of patience to be of service to our frightened neighbors—not the least being President Bush. Help us and help him to be what we say we are—Christians. Amen.

Aldersgate Sermons

Normalcy. God, how we want to return to normalcy. We feel a bit guilty about our desire for the everyday, but you can only live on the razor's edge so long. They say the events of September 11th have forever changed our world, but if that is so what are we doing here in this class? That we can "take up where we left off" surely is a sign that life can and should get back to normal. We have families to tend, churches to serve, and we must eat. How can we do that in the face of the horror? Remind us, Lord of time, that you have made it possible in a world of tragedy to keep on keeping on because the world really was changed at Golgotha. In Jesus' cross, you pulled us into your surprising kingdom, making us, forcing us, to see the extraordinary character of the everyday. In the face of the crucifixion, you give us time to love one another. So, by all means, we pray that your Spirit will guide us through the everyday, making possible our living in your peace in a world of war.

Christ the King: Thanksgiving

II Samuel 23: 1-7
Revelation 1: 4-8
John 18: 33-38

"My kingdom is not from this world." Few sentences from the Bible have caused more trouble for Christians than this one. Our rush to take comfort in the claim that Jesus' kingship is not of this world is the source of an infinite variety of Christian unfaithfulness to the Gospel. We think, for example, that with these words Jesus anticipates the distinction between religion and politics necessary to sustain our assumption that religion and politics do not or should not mix. Some have even argued that Jesus' claim that his kingdom is not of this world makes Jesus the founder of democratic social orders, at least to the extent that such orders depend on the distinction between church and state. We, therefore, assume that it is appropriate at Thanksgiving to give thanks for this nation because America is the fruit of Jesus' confrontation with Pilate.

I have to tell you, however, that Jesus would find our thanksgiving for this nation problematic. He would do so to the extent that America names the attempt to avoid recognizing that Jesus is King. It is hard for us to understand that we stand with Pilate before Jesus because we think we have little use for any king. After all, does America not name the end of kingship language in favor of the rule of the people? Were we not taught from grade school on that the American Revolution was justified because the American people rightly wanted no king to rule them? Kingships, after all, are arbitrary forms of government left behind by enlightened and rational people like us. We are a people who are ruled only by ourselves expressed through our chosen representatives.

That, of course, results in one minor problem: Jesus does not want to be our democratically elected leader. Indeed, he is quite insistent that we do not get to choose him. He gets to elect us. He is, after all, the heir to David's throne. David, moreover, was every inch a king chosen not by the people but by God. To be sure, the kingship in Israel proved to be an ambiguous gift, as kings have a habit of forgetting that they are chosen by God—as we hear in the book of Samuel—to "rule over people justly, ruling in the fear of God." Nevertheless, the Davidic kings of Israel were rulers given by God for the care of God's people Israel. Moreover, if that kingship had ended for Israel, there is no question that Jesus reclaimed that role for himself. Only now, he is king not only of Israel but also of all creation.

So, it seems we are stuck with this kingship language. We cannot deny that Jesus is a king; after all, he was crowned with thorns and given a purple robe. That Jesus is undeniably a king has led to thousands of bad sermons trying to explain to a democratic people how to avoid the obvious. Thus, we have been told that what it means for Jesus to be King is that he is the Lord of our hearts. Or, what it means for Jesus to be King is that our ultimate loyalties must finally be to God. The only problem with such claims is that we have no idea how we might know what it means for Jesus to be Lord of our hearts or our ultimate loyalty. We Christians, for example, have been more than willing to kill other Christians in the name of loyalty to democratically elected leaders, all the while thinking that our ultimate loyalty was to Jesus.

If you think that all Jesus meant by claiming kingship is that he wants to rule each individual's heart, then how did he get himself killed? There must have been some terrible miscommunication between Jesus and Pontius Pilate. Admittedly, Pilate seems not to have wanted to kill Jesus. Pilate clearly thought he was no more than another Jewish nut. Yet, we are told that when it was pointed out to Pilate that Jesus did not disavow being a king—Jesus had, after all, observed that Pilate himself called him a king—this meant that he was the enemy of the emperor and accordingly should be killed. Pilate did his duty, as he should have if he was to be a servant of the emperor. So, Jesus was rightly killed with the inscription written in Hebrew, Latin, and Greek, "The King of the Jews"—a King, accordingly, who reigned over all people.

Emperors, even democratically elected emperors, will always kill those who claim their title. "Render unto Caesar the things that are Caesar's and unto God the things that are God's" is not good news for those who would be Caesar. Caesar wants it all. We may think Caesar can have our bodies while we reserve our hearts and loyalties for God, but do not forget that our hearts are also flesh. We distinguish between the public and the private, thinking that Caesar rules the public but God rules in the private parts of our lives. Yet, the distinction between the public and the private turns out to be a distinction that hides from us how thoroughly we are ruled by the rulers of this world.

Notice that everything depends on how we understand "world." I fear that too often we read, "My kingdom is not from this world," without reading the next sentence. Jesus says, "If my kingdom were from this world, my followers would be fighting to keep me from being handed over to the Jews. But as it is, my kingdom is not from here." Notice that when Jesus denies that his kingdom is "from this world," he does not disavow the rule, a kingdom, which he does represent. Rather, he says that his kingdom is not one that will triumph through violence, but it is no less a kingdom because of that disavowal.

I sometimes joke with my friends who defend Christian participation in war by using just war criteria that, surely, if war is justified in defense of the innocent, the disciples should have rushed back to Galilee and mobilized the Galilean liberation front to rescue Jesus from the cross. After all, if Jesus' execution were not an example of injustice, then it would be hard to know what counted for injustice. Indeed, one of my favorite stories is about my cousin, Billy Dick, when he was about six. He was in a Sunday School class in which he was usually appropriately bored, but one Sunday the teacher told about the crucifixion of Jesus. Suddenly, Billy Dick was energized and raised his hand to speak. The teacher finally called on Billy Dick, who stood up and declared, in the language he had learned from his bricklaying family, "If Gene Autry had been there, the dirty SOB's would not have gotten away with it!" I suspect we think that if we had been there, we might have tried to prevent Jesus from going to the cross. We would have done so, however, as agents of the emperor who feared this kind of king.

Jesus is no less political for declaring that his followers do not use the sword in defense of the Kingdom of God. Yet, if they do not use the sword, what weapon do they have? "Pilate asked him, 'So you are a king?' Jesus answered, 'You say that I am a king. For this I was born, and for this I came into the world, to testify to the truth. Everyone who belongs to the truth listens to my voice.'" Truth is our weapon. Truth is the only alternative to the politics of the sword. Truth, of course, takes time. However, we believe that through the cross and resurrection of Christ God has given us all the time in the world to be God's truth for the world, for without us, without those who confess that our King is this Jesus, the world cannot know that there is an alternative to the violence of the world.

In the book of Revelation we are identified as those who are made by Jesus' blood into a kingdom, "priests serving his God and Father." We are able to be such a kingdom because Jesus Christ was "the faithful witness, the firstborn of the dead, and the ruler of the kings of the earth." The "ruler of the kings of the earth" is not exactly a ruler who only wants to rule over our personal lives. The rulers of this world are deadly, gaining their power from our fear of death; but this King Jesus has conquered death, making possible our being a people that is able to say "no" to worldly power. For Jesus is God, the Alpha and the Omega, who alone is able to unleash into the world his church, the foretaste of his kingdom, a wild people who refuse to be ruled even by those who claim to rule on our behalf.

What could be more appropriate, therefore, than to end the church year, a year that began by our learning to wait with Israel for the Messiah, with the Feast of Christ the King. In truth, this is a recent feast day. Pius XI established the Feast of Christ the King in 1925 with the encyclical *Quas primas*. He did so as a response to the horror of World War I. He began the encyclical bluntly, asserting that the only source of renewal for war-torn Europe depended on the public recognition and celebration of the kingship of Christ. Pius XI acknowledged that "Christ the King" has often been interpreted metaphorically, that is, that Christ exercises reign over our minds, our wills, and our hearts. Yet, he observed, "If we ponder this matter more deeply," we cannot but see that the title and power of King belong to Christ who was, as Chalcedon maintains, fully God and fully man. Therefore, just as God is fully embodied in this man, so also his kingdom must be embodied politically. That is why Pius XI rightly thought that we, God's church, are the alternative to a world of war.

If Christ is not King, then what we do when we bury our brother, Herb, is a lie, for then his life—a life that had the time in a world without time to take time to love the beauty of each flower and each of us—would not make sense.[14] Lives like Herb's are our politics of resistance against the politics of the lie. Moreover, what we do today when we baptize Alice would be false if Christ had not conquered death. The death in which Alice will be baptized is Christ's death, a death that brings life, making possible our participation in God's politics as an alternative to the politics of death that rules the world. Our celebration of Herb's life and death and this baptism are essential acts that determine our politics as the church of Christ.

The politics that the church is stands as an alternative to the politics determined by the fear of death that characterizes the world. The politics of the world, the politics of Pontius Pilate, can only result in violence against those who would expose the lies on which the emperor relies for legitimacy. That is why, as we heard in Revelation, we are not just a people who proclaim the good news of Christ, but we are the good news of Christ. We are such because we have been elected to be the people of God, David's people, by the one alone who has the right to declare to the world that Jesus is King.

---

[14] Herb was the husband of our Pastor.

Aldersgate Sermons

Lord Jesus Christ, we live in a world without lords. We have presidents, but they rule with our consent—or at least this is the story we tell ourselves. We believe that just as we claim to govern, so we govern our own lives. We are not set up to use "Lord" language. So, do you mind if we call you "Mr. President," Jesus? That, we confess, sounds strange. You did not and do not act like you are running for office. Driving money changers out of the temple seems a bit beyond the pale. What is worse, at the wedding at Cana you were a bit short with your mother, and it is even more troubling you never married and spent most of your time with a bunch of guys. We worry a bit if you ever came to terms with your sexuality. When all is said and done, we do not think you are going to be elected for president.

So, what are we doing to do with you, Lord Jesus Christ? We confess that we do not have the slightest idea. All we can do is pray that you will destroy our presumption that we are our own lords. We fear such destruction, sensing that it may have something to do with death, and as Yoder tells us, in the life and death of Jesus we find a reality and the possibility of all that your teachings say. It is possible to live that way if you are willing to die that way. Is that really part of what it means to call you Lord? I guess this means we have to get serious when we haven't the slightest idea of what it might mean to get serious.

For God's sake, dear Jesus, Lord Jesus, help us.

Disrupting Time

Another day, another death. Should we get used to this, dear Christ, used to death that dribbles rather than pours? Please help us remain alive to the everyday deaths of those in Iraq. In this impossible situation for American soldiers and Iraqis may they see you in one another. Help us not lose sight of the fears and loves that led our leaders to create this terror. Give them and us souls expanded by your Spirit to see a way forward that is not just another day and another death. In the between time, we pray for the end of war, for the end of terror, for the end of killing. Make us that end.

Aldersgate Sermons

Another day, another death. An American soldier dies in an ambush—we register the death as unreal. Dear God, we pray for the end of killing. We do so without much hope that the killing will end. It does not seem all that bad, just one or two a day. Abstract deaths in an abstract war. Yet, we know that those who die and those who kill are not an abstraction to you. Make those who die and those who kill real for us so that we might join one another in that long mourners' bench called history. How long, how long, Lord, will this killing continue? Make us incapable of "getting used to it." Make us burn with the passion of your peace; fire our imaginations with your love, so that we might work to find alternatives to war by being an alternative to war. May we learn to fear you more than we fear one another and so fearing become for the world your trust.

Disrupting Time

For God's sake, God, why can you not grant us vengeance? Can you not feel the pain, the terror, the horror of murder? Can you not recognize the emptiness left in the wake of murder? We want, we desperately desire, to have our world rid of those who kill without regret. We join our voices with the Psalmist for vengeance, for the recovery of the world. Eye for eye, but it is not "our" world. It is your world. Vengeance, it turns out, is yours not ours. It seems, moreover, that you will not trust us with your vengeance. After all, it was vengeance that killed your son—a killing that forever ended our attempts to make our world safe by more killing. A hard lesson not easily learned. So, we continue to kill in the name of vengeance, in the name of safety. Make us, your church, desire not safety, but the justice of your Son's cross. May we be for the world the embodiment of the justice shaped by charity, found continually present in the Eucharist—the end of all sacrifice. Through that sacrifice, make us a people who would rather die than kill. So made, may we be the end of capital punishment.

Heirs
by Paula Gilbert

Matthew 21:33-46

"This is the heir; come, let us kill him and get his inheritance."

You may have noticed, I daresay, a certain heavy-handedness on the part of Matthew in recounting this incident. Just in case someone in his audience doesn't know the broad overview of God's dealings with the Jews beginning with Moses and continuing through the prophets, just in case someone doesn't know how the Jews responded to God over the centuries since Moses, Matthew makes it about as clear as one can make any point. "When the chief priests and the Pharisees heard his parables," asserts Matthew, "they realized that he was speaking about them. They wanted to arrest Jesus, but they feared the crowd, because they regarded him as a prophet."

With Matthew being so up front, so plainspoken, so definitive, so obvious, the story Jesus tells is revealed not to be a parable, but more of a metaphor or an allegory. God is the landowner who plants a vineyard in the most careful and prudent of ways. But, having planted the vineyard and secured it, the landowner leases the vineyard to certain tenants who are the Jews. Harvest time comes, and the landowner decides to claim his yield of the harvest. So, the landowner, that is God, sends slaves to claim the produce—not once but twice. But, both times the slaves, who are the spokespersons of God, the prophets of God—both times the slaves are rejected, and beaten, and killed. So, the landowner sends a third time to claim the produce of the vineyard. And this time the landowner, or God, sends his son, his heir—God sends Jesus. Yet, the response of the tenants of the vineyard is no different, and when they see the son they say to themselves, "This is the heir; come, let us kill him and get his inheritance." And they kill the son. They kill Jesus.

When we hear the story this way, there is but one conclusion we can draw, and it is a conclusion the text seems to provide for us. Matthew says that Jesus announces, "Therefore I tell you, the kingdom of God will be taken away from you and given to a people that produces the fruits of the kingdom." Not surprisingly, one early Christian interpretation of the meaning of this text is that the promises of God to the Jews have been transferred, in the light of Jesus' death, from the Jews to the Church.

This is not, however, the only interpretation the Church has given to this so-called parable, this "parable of the wicked tenants" as it is referred to in the New Revised Standard Version. Indeed, the title—"parable of the wicked tenants"—is a subheading that modern translators and scholars have inserted into the gospel to divide it into segments for easier reading, and to give to us, the readers, a phrase to spark our memory of the passage. In entitling this passage "the parable of the wicked servants," our modern-day scripture scholars intend to help us claim this story as our story, as a story that speaks to us now and explains who we are in reference to God and God's vineyard.

And so, this interpretation goes something like this. Now we are the tenants of this carefully designed vineyard that the landowner, that God, has established. And, in the landowner's absence, we are the ones who day in and day out, month in and month out—we are the ones who prune and fertilize and water the vines. We are the ones who watch the fruit develop, who guard the transformation from flower, to green and hard unripened fruit, and finally to soft and luscious grapes. We are the ones who work for the harvest, and we believe that the harvest by right is ours because we are the ones who have labored for it. We wish to possess the vineyard. We wish to claim the harvest as our own. We become arrogant. We want to possess God's kingdom, and we claim it as our own because we are the ones whose labors secure the harvest. In another day and in another age we kill Christ again in order to seize Christ's inheritance. We are the proud and mighty Church.

To put ourselves in the story as the tenants and to hear the passage in this way is to hear this parable of the wicked tenants as a parable about ourselves and the pride we take in our accomplishments as individual Christians, as congregations, as denominations, as Roman Catholics and Protestants, as the Church. When we recognize that we are the wicked tenants, then Jesus says to us, "Therefore I tell you, the kingdom of God will be taken away from you and given to a people that produces the fruits of the kingdom." The call to us, the message of the parable to us who have ears to hear it is a call to repentance, to turn around and turn back, and to remember that we are only tenants of the vineyard. We do not possess God's kingdom. We have only been called to labor faithfully in it and for it.

This morning I wish to suggest to you yet another interpretation of this parable, a third interpretation, if you will. It is a haunting interpretation I cannot avoid reaching when I ponder the plot of the tenants summed up in this sentence: "This is the heir; come, let us kill him and get his inheritance." You see, the truth of the matter is that we did kill the heir. Not the priests, not the scribes, not the Pharisees—not the Jews and not the Romans—we are the ones who kill the heir. When Pilate asks us whom he should free, we choose Barabbas. We choose that Barabbas be freed, and we choose that Jesus be crucified. Judas betrays him, the priests arrest him, the soldiers drive the nails through his hands and raise him on the cross. But, it is the word we speak, it is the choice we make, that hangs Jesus there. The irony is this: we kill him, and yet we do receive his inheritance.

Through his death, we are given life. Through faith in Jesus Christ, we are delivered from our captivity to sin and death.

But, there is even more to this matter of the inheritance, I think—a kind of irony on top of irony. We kill the Son and we get the inheritance—and, in turn, we become the heirs. We become the heirs, the sons and daughters, sent to the vineyard, sent into the world, sent to claim the harvest for God. We are heirs not only of the glory, heirs not only of Jesus' promises, heirs not only of Christ's riches, but we are also heirs of the Son's mission. We inherit freedom from sin and death; we inherit, too, the responsibility to seek the lost, to proclaim the good news, to be the sacrifice of God re-presented to the world in every age and in every place.

Disrupting Time

Our inheritance is to be killed that God might claim the world through us who are the heirs of God's only Son.

Herbert and Mary Zigbuo have been sent to Liberia and to the Ivory Coast. We are sent to Chapel Hill and to Durham and to Carrboro and to the Research Triangle Park and to Raleigh. We are sent to schools and companies and to neighborhoods to claim God's harvest. We are sent not for the glory but for the mission. We are sent to serve. We are sent, perhaps, to be betrayed, to be deserted, to be killed. We are sent to be God's voices crying in the wilderness of modern life. We are sent as the heirs of Jesus, the Son, the Christ.

But, we are not sent alone, nor are we sent without provisions for our journey. We gather today and every Sunday because we need the illumination of God's word, we need the people, we need the nourishment of heavenly food and drink. When we come to this table this morning, we come to receive the food and drink that feeds us with the body and blood of our Lord—the body and blood that unites us with him, with his life, and with his mission. We come to feast at the table of our Lord. And, from the table we rise and go forth to claim the vineyard, to claim the world as God's own.

On this particular day—this World Communion Sunday—we do not come only with those whom we see in this place, but we come with that vast army of God that stretches across all time and stretches to every place. We come as servants, and we come as heirs. We come so that we may receive God's grace that is so abundant in this holy sacrament. We come so that we may be transformed by that grace and so live in the world as faithful and courageous heirs of our heavenly Lord.

"This is the heir; come, let us kill him and get his inheritance."

Thanks be to God who forgives us our sin.

Thanks be to God who incorporates us into the kingdom and makes us fellow heirs with Christ Jesus.

Thanks be to God who calls us to produce the fruits of righteousness for the harvest of God's kingdom.

Thanks be to God.

From Bennettsville, South Carolina
to Scotland and
Chapel Hill, North Carolina

Witnesses against Ourselves
A Sermon at First Presbyterian Church
Bennettsville, South Carolina
Sunday, November 10, 2002

Joshua 24: 1-3, 14-25
I Thessalonians 4: 13-18
Matthew 25: 1-13

Decisive decisions are seldom noticed when we make them. Often, we are not even aware we have made a decision, and we definitely do not realize that what we have chosen makes a decisive difference. Only as we look back do such decisions seem to be momentous. I think this is true not only in our personal lives, but also for institutions and communities. For example, I suspect that at the time when many of us decide to go or not to go to college we have little sense of the significance such a decision will have for the rest of our lives. Those who decide to go to college only retrospectively appreciate the influence this or that particular school has had on their lives. Indeed, I suspect that it tells us a good deal about who we are that often where we went to school determines to a greater degree who we become than where we went or did not go to church when we were in college.

It may be even harder for institutions to know when they are facing a decisive decision at the time the decision is actually made. Indeed, often, decisive decisions do not even feel like decisions. Institutions—or rather those charged with responsibility for maintaining institutions—tend to be conservative, for institutions embody hard won habits for survival forged by the challenges of the past. The temptation is always to trust the known, fearing as we do the uncertainty of the unknown. Yet, to trust the known when everything around you is changing means that even the known is transformed into something different than it was. The problem, both personally and institutionally, is seldom whether we should or should not change, but rather how to account for how we remain the same either as a person or institution amid the constant change that constitutes our lives.

Institutions often die or at least become irrelevant by trusting in the decisive decisions made in the past. For example, Methodism, at least for a while, became the dominant form of mainstream Protestantism in America because of the itinerancy system. The Methodists could follow the American people west because anyone called to the Methodist ministry knew he or she was a person on the move. Accordingly, extraordinary men (and it was at that time largely men) were called to the Methodist ministry because they saw that ministry as an ongoing challenge. To be a Methodist minister was to accept a life of uncertainty, and that is why so many found such a life so fulfilling—they usually died young.

Methodists continue to cling to the itinerancy system, though now that system no longer represents a life of challenge but just the opposite. That is, itinerancy now means guaranteed employment. I had just come to teach in the Divinity School at Duke when a friend called me to see how I was doing. I told him I was depressed. I thought at first that the depression might be just personal challenges. But, the more I thought about it, I realized that what was depressing me was the Methodist church. I noted that I had come to the Divinity School assuming that the primary challenge would be to form students that were angry about the unfaithful accommodation of the Methodist church to American culture. My job, I thought, would be to say, "Of course the church has been unfaithful, but it is still God's church, and your task is to serve the church patiently and without compromise."

I observed to my friend, however, that I did not find that kind of student at Duke (though I am happy to say that our students have changed). Instead, I found students who were supremely happy with the current character of Methodism and, in particular, with the current expectations of the ministry. Itinerancy, rather than offering a life of insecurity, now represented lifelong security. To be a successful Methodist minister all you have to do is be nice and have a fairly pleasant personality and every four years you will be moved to a larger church with an increase in pay. To be in the Methodist ministry is a little like being in the military. After you have been through boot camp, you will be taken care of for the rest of your life. The main difference is that the life of a soldier still has some danger to keep it interesting, all of which means that the Methodists have the illusion that they are being faithful to the itinerancy system even though that system now no longer does the work it originally performed.

In our text from Joshua, we find a people confronted by a decisive decision. The great judge Joshua, Moses' assistant, whom God called to lead the people during the confusing time when they made their way into the promised land, calls the leaders of the people to Shechem. He begins by reminding the people of all that God has done for them, not the least benefit being that they know that their God is not the gods of their ancestors. Joshua observes that when Terah and his sons Abraham and Nahor lived beyond the Euphrates, they served other gods. In order for Abraham to know God, it was necessary for him to leave his country to sojourn in the land of Canaan. The calling of Abraham was, of course, but the beginning of God's great deeds with Israel, not the least being the Exodus. God has even given them "a land on which you had not labored, and towns that you had not built, and you live in them; you eat the fruit of vineyards and olive yards that you did not plant." Israel is Israel because God is Israel's God.

Yet, there seems to be a problem. The gods of Israel's forebears keep hanging around. It is, after all, hard to give up on what has worked in the past. But God tells Joshua that he is to force a decision, a decisive decision: "Choose this day whom you will serve"—the gods of your ancestors or the Lord. The people answer that the last thing in the world they would want to do is serve the old gods, the gods of their ancestors in the region beyond the river, so they choose the God who has done all these great things for them. However, Joshua is not convinced that the people understand the decisive nature of this decision, so he reminds them that the Lord is a holy and jealous God who will not forgive their transgressions or sin. "If you forsake the Lord and serve foreign gods, then he will turn and do you harm, and consume you, after having done you good."

Again, the people say, "No problem. We have this thing figured out. Keep the gifts coming and you can trust us," but Joshua remains unconvinced, observing, "You are witnesses against yourselves that you have chosen the Lord, to serve him." The people respond, "We are witnesses." The Bible, generally thought not to be a book noted for the use of irony, seems here to suggest ironically that the people are witnesses against themselves. They have been confronted with a decisive decision, but they continue to fail to see just what makes such a decision so decisive.

I suspect, however, that we cannot help but feel some sympathy with the people of Israel when confronted by Joshua. As I noted, it is hard to know when a decisive decision is before us, particularly when it comes to knowing which god we serve. Moreover, we know that the continuing history of the people of Israel is one of unfaithfulness and God's unrelenting desire to have Israel as his promised people. Israel's faithfulness is perhaps nowhere better manifest than in her willingness to tell the story of her unfaithfulness. That is an extraordinary achievement that is a reminder that Israel never forgot that her story is the story of God's faithfulness: it is an important reminder that the main character in the Old Testament is God.

I think that we should also feel some sympathy with those confronted by Joshua's challenge, because the current challenge facing us as Christians in the world in which we find ourselves is not unlike that suggested by our text for today. Indeed, in some ways our situation is worse. We are confident that we have made the decisive decision about which god we worship. We feel no reason to think we need to rethink our decision to worship the God of Abraham, Moses, and Joshua. That same God, we believe, has made us inheritors of the promise to Israel through the cross and resurrection of Christ.

But, I fear that like the five foolish bridesmaids who kept no oil for their lamps, bridesmaids who failed to see that our Savior is an apocalyptic Lord, we are not ready for the bridegroom. We have allowed ourselves to believe that we are Christians, so we know what God we are worshiping. Yet, the god we worship too often turns out to be a god who is useful to us, rather than the God who judges nations and empires. David Yeago, a Lutheran theologian who teaches at the Lutheran seminary in Columbia, South Carolina, observes that the church in modernity exists in a "ceaseless crisis of legitimation."[15] By this, Yeago means that the church bears the burden of proof. For the church to be legitimate, to justify its reason for being, the church has to show that it serves some purposes good for the larger order of which it is but a part—for example, "The family that prays together stays together." It is assumed that the church has jurisdiction only over the private parts of our lives, which means at best that the church provides the motivational factors necessary for us to do what we assume is good to do whether we are Christians or not. The religious right and the religious left both want to highjack the church for their own interests. The right wants God to bless the American government as the only "godly government" ever known; the left wants God to be on their side in peace and justice issues.

Yeago points out that the other possibility for the church to legitimate herself is by being the supplier of goods and services to consumers. He notes that it is not difficult to understand why this is an attractive alternative for mainline churches because if the churches meet "religious needs," then the church at least has some idea of what it is for. The problem with this strategy is that the market is governed by the principle of subjective value, that is, goods and services have whatever value consumers choose. When the church becomes the supplier of religious needs, we cannot help but become people who say they worship the God of Israel, when, in fact, we remain captive to the gods of our former homeland.

Yeago observes that it is easy to deride church-growth marketers for their crassness. Indeed, there seems to be no limit to their willingness to subject God to the market. For example, I have a brochure advertising promotional kits to get people back in the church on the first anniversary of September 11, 2001, which asks the provocative question: "Is your church ready for an outreach event that may rival Easter?" Yet, we let ourselves off too easily if we distance ourselves from such strategies only because they are crass. The attempt, Yeago argues, to market God and the church only draws on habits characteristic of mainline Protestantism, which assumes that the only account of the God we worship that will be acceptable to modern people is one in which God insures that we will not have to suffer because we worship the one true God.

---

[15]David Yeago's observations are to be found in "Messiah's People: The Culture of the Church in the Midst of the Nations," *Pro Ecclesia* 6/1: 146-170.

So, I am bold enough to say that I believe that Christians in America face the kind of decisive decision demanded by Joshua. "Choose this day whom you will serve" is not a decision that we can assume has already been made, but rather one (just as that we must be prepared with enough oil) that always remains before God's people. Indeed, the challenge is even more dreadful once we realize that we, the baptized, do not stand before Joshua, but rather that God has called us, God's church, to be Joshua for the world. We are to be the kind of people who make clear to the world that there is a choice between having our lives ruled by the gods created by our desires and the holy and jealous God of Israel. That God, the God of Israel, has given us his law, his Christ, so that we may discover when we are leading lives that fail to acknowledge God is God and we are not.

The standard ending for a sermon on this famous passage from Joshua is to ask us to decide which god we will serve, but for us that would only result in another consumer choice. Rather, I suggest that we pray God to lead us into a land that makes our worship of the old gods apparent. That "land," that "place," we believe to be found in the celebration of the Eucharist, in which God makes us part of his sacrifice for the world. The Eucharist is God's gift, which comes not from our own labor or vineyards we have planted. The Eucharist is God's decisive decision for the world. It is the stone God has erected that at once judges and saves us—saved because we are judged. So, let us pray that unfaithful as we are, God may use us to be witnesses against ourselves so that the world may know that our God is God.

From Bennettsville, South Carolina to Scotland

Gentle us, gentle savior. I am tempted by unrighteous anger to make these students as angry as I am. I comfort my angry self with insight. Anger, after all, is not unknown among those we call your saints. I fear that my anger comes not from charity, but pretensions and pride. I say that I want to love you and yours, but I despise those smooth lives that claim the name Christian. So, I pray, dear God, that you shake my anger, our anger, by your harsh and dreadful love, making us people who shine with the confidence that comes from being made your people.

Disrupting Time

Gentle savior, gentle me. I am tempted to turn your touch into anger. Anger that knows no end. Anger that gives me existence, a place to be different. I know that I cannot will my way free of anger. So, help me see and hear your good gift to us in the embrace of the morning bird's song that testifies to how wonderful it is to be alive. Make me as glad to be alive as that bird, to enjoy the interruptions of your kingdom called friends, and to rejoice in the sheer there-ness of existence. Discipline my anger by the gift of joy that comes by being made your friends through the body and blood of your son, our Lord, Jesus Christ.

From Bennettsville, South Carolina to Scotland

Prayer before "debate" with Paige Paterson

Contentious Lord, God knows you must love a good argument. How else are we to explain the people of your promise, the Jews? Moreover, you have told us that our salvation comes from those argumentative people, a people threatened by the world, yet refusing to be distracted from their arguments with you and one another concerning the faithful living of your law. Teach us, the grateful people, to love your Word, that we, like the Jews, may argue our way into loving you and one another. Argument, it seems, is your salvation—an alternative to the violence of the world.

But, as we contend together, save us from pride and the vanity pride nourishes. Remind us that it is not a matter of winning, but rather of the up-building of your church, the body of Christ. Too long divided, help us glimpse as we contend with one another the unity of your church. Indeed, make us your witness so that the world, observing how we argue, will say, "See how they love one another; they would rather argue than kill."

"God symbolizes that structure of experience that gives meaning and value to the whole human experience because God transcends every particular experience in a unity of experience. The God-symbol conceptually enacts the unification of every reality—reality being the indifferentiated totality of experience. God signifies the union of all life with concrete actuality and ideal potentiality. Therefore, the idea of God designates the totality of meaning and value. As the American philosopher at the turn of the century, Josiah Royce, once proposed, God simply is the world. 'God symbolizes an unrestricted field of value whose harmony involves an ever-enlarging process of synthesis of the widest range and deepest contrast of relational data,' says Nancy Frankenberry."[16]

Savior God, Father of our Lord Jesus Christ, Wild Spirit, I confess that when I read these words I was filled with pride. What absolute and complete shit. If you are not more than the "structure of experience," then what in the world is prayer? Is this the God "before whom we shall have no others?" Is this the "One who raised Jesus from the dead, having before raised Israel from Egypt?" Is this the End for which all creation groans? Rhetorical questions, but are they prayer? Probably not, if they are not more than a weapon against those who write of you as "symbol."

So, I must pray that you destroy my pride and anger. Make me, make all of us, humble before the mystery that is you. That you have given us your name tempts us to believe that we know who you are. That we think you are a "who" and not a "what" can even lead us to think that you exist for no other reason than for our desires. So, we praise you; we bless you; we sing to you the song of Mary, so that we may be like her—your handmaid. Humble us, and so humbled may we be so enthralled by you that no one is ever tempted to think of you as "symbol."

---

[16]Victor Anderson, "Contour of an African American Public Theology," *Journal of Theology* (Dayton: United Theological Seminary, 2000), 57-58.

Providential Peace
A Sermon at St. Salvator's Chapel, St. Andrews
For Sunday, February 18, 2001

Genesis 45: 3-11, 15
I Corinthians 15: 35-38, 42-50
Luke 6: 27-38

In a philosophy class at Duke, Alasdair MacIntyre made reference to the Genesis account of God's command to Abraham to sacrifice Isaac. I do not know the context, but it may well have involved a discussion of Kierkegaard. A student raised his hand, confessing that he had no idea what MacIntyre was talking about because he had never heard that story. So, MacIntyre spelled out what God had asked Abraham to do. The student was still dissatisfied and asked MacIntyre how the story came out. MacIntyre responded, "We do not yet know."

I do not know whether this is a true story if you mean by true that "it really happened." But, I do know that it is the kind of story, which, even if it did not happen, is too good not to be true. Moreover, it is a story that I think has everything to do with our texts for this morning. MacIntyre's response, "We do not yet know," interestingly enough challenges some of the basic presumptions that make it difficult for us to understand the Joseph story, for the Joseph story requires us to believe that the past—what we often call history—can be redeemed. The past can be reclaimed because we do not yet know what it means for it to be the past until it has been redeemed. The classical Christian word to describe this understanding of history—and I cannot believe I must use this word in Scotland—is providence.

Unlike MacIntyre's student, I suspect that most of us know the Joseph story well enough. After all, the Joseph story comes closer to being a short novel than any text in the Bible other than the successionist narrative in Samuel. Indeed, I suspect that most of us are fairly sympathetic with Joseph's brothers because not only was Joseph given special treatment by his father, Jacob, but Joseph also assumed that he deserved the coat he wore. So, we almost think, "Good riddance," when the brothers throw him in a pit and then sell him. He ends up in Egypt where his dreams give him a leg up on the social policy engineers of his day. He becomes the Pharaoh's right-hand man, making possible his generous response to his starving brothers. Of course, he first tests them to see if they will treat Benjamin in the same manner they had treated him.

Moved by Judah's willingness to become a slave so that Benjamin could return to Jacob, Joseph reveals that he is the very brother they sold into slavery. But, he is not angry, because "God sent me before you to preserve for you a remnant on earth, and to keep alive for you many survivors. So it was not you who sent me here, but God." Or, more dramatically, in the last chapter of the book of Genesis Joseph declares, "Do not be afraid! Am I in the place of God? Even though you intended to do harm to me, God intended it for good, in order to preserve a numerous people, as he is doing today" (50: 19-20).

I think that these are extremely dangerous texts for a people who at least once believed that the Reformed Church of Scotland was the climax of God's providential care of the world. A few years ago when I was in Aberdeen, Iain Torrance told me that if I wanted to understand Scotland, I must read John Buchan's wonderful novel, *Witch Wood*. I did so, and I was shocked at what I discovered. I knew that, at least at one time, Reformed ministers thought Scotland was like Israel. I simply had no idea they thought that Scotland was Israel, which, I think, is but a reminder that we should not confuse God's providential care with the quasi-Stoic presumption that providence means that in the long run everything will work out for the best. I love the land and the people that constitute Scotland, but I do not think that the climax of God's creation is Scotland. The jury is still out on Texas.

From Bennettsville, South Carolina to Scotland

In fact, everything did not work out for the best for Israel. The tribes of Israel, through Joseph's good office, dwelled in Egypt. But, a Pharaoh arose who did not know Joseph, with the result that the people of Israel were enslaved. Joseph's protection of his people led to their subjugation. This is no success story, which is surely one of the reasons that the Joseph story, and in particular the passage from the last chapter of Genesis, was and continues to be one of the texts most favored by the African-American church. Captured and enslaved, cruelly treated, subjugated by Christians, African-Americans believe that God intended it for good. But, the good is not a success story; rather, it is the miracle that the most nearly faithful form of Christianity in America was formed in the souls of slaves.

This is but a reminder that providence is not about how things work out for us. Providence is about how the God of Israel and Jesus Christ will not be denied, for this God is able to redeem the past not by turning failure into success, but by refusing to allow our sinfulness to determine God's unrelenting desire to save us. Our belief in God's providence is not an invitation to speculate or, worse, act as if we can anticipate what God's future will be. Insofar as we are able to name how God has providentially cared for us, we do so only retrospectively. Surely, that is why Israel best remembered the Joseph stories in exile.

Yet, I think, we must acknowledge that we—that is, all who have been constituted by modernity—simply have no way to comprehend God's providence. We do not believe in providence. We believe in history. That is, we do not believe that our forebears are Abraham and Joseph, but rather that we are in community only with those with whom we share temporal contiguity. We can figuratively "play-at" being Abraham's offspring, but real history is constituted by a naturalistic chain of cause and effect synchronically exemplified by clock and calendar.[17]

I think it sobering but nonetheless important for us to acknowledge that for Augustine or Calvin or Barth, God's providence—the story in which we participate by God's grace—is more real, more truthful, than what we call history. For Augustine, Calvin, and Barth, we are Abraham's

---

[17] I am indebted to my friend, Professor Scott Bader-Saye, who teaches at the University of Scranton, and in particular his paper, "Providence, Peacemaking, and Patience: Or How Providence Became History," recently delivered at the Society of Christian Ethics, for this way of putting the matter.

children, spared death by the ram called Christ, more than we are (as we often say) products of history. That we cannot even imagine what it might mean to be Abraham's children can be illustrated by how tentatively I make and you receive the suggestion that Abraham's willingness to sacrifice Isaac foreshadows God's sacrifice of his Son on the cross. We have been taught not to impose Christian "meanings" on the text of the Old Testament, failing to realize that we would not even have an Old Testament if the evangelists and Paul had not thought it possible to see Christ in the Old Testament. If, in other words, Christ is not the key that finally makes sense of Joseph's declaration, "You intended to do harm to me, God intended it for good, in order to preserve a numerous people, as he is doing today," then the God we come to worship today is not God.

We cannot deny, however, that we live on the presumption that history and not providence rules our lives. That is why, for example, what we do here when we worship God has the feel of unreality, which leads us to wonder what our worship has to do with the rest of our lives. I am not trying to make us feel guilty for not trusting in God's providence, but rather to indicate that our inability to imagine what it might mean to live as if Abraham is our father means that we have been captured by a very different politics than the politics of the church. In his extraordinary book, *Torture and Eucharist*, Bill Cavanaugh observes, "The production of the nation-state depends especially on people imagining themselves contemporaries not with the apostles and the saints, but with all the other presently living French (or Chileans or English)" (223). That is why, as Hegel observed, "Newspapers serve modern man as a substitute for prayer."[18] For, newspapers and history are written from and underwrite the presumption that the way things are is the way things have to be. Accordingly, the past cannot be redeemed because the past at best but names what we need to know to understand the present, a present that, we are sure, is more determined by nations and empires than the church of Jesus Christ.

This is why the Gospel for today cannot help but strike us as a worthy ideal but impossible to live. I confess that I am almost tempted to think it is providential that I stand before you today obligated to preach on these

---

[18] Again, I am indebted to Bader-Saye for the association of history and Hegel's observation about the role of newspapers.

texts assigned by the lectionary. I am a pacifist, and I assume that most of you are not. I could not have asked for better texts to justify my commitment to nonviolence. These are texts I can now use to beat you over the head for not being nonviolent. That's an unworthy game, I fear, one often played, which leaves none of us any wiser. I, of course, do want you to live lives of nonviolence, but to so live is unintelligible, indeed unimaginable, if God does not care providentially for creation.

What can I possibly mean by such a claim? First, consider how we respond to Jesus' commands that we love our enemies, do good to those who hate us, offer the other cheek to those who strike us, give to those who beg. No one, I believe, can resist responding to Jesus' commands with the thought, "This is just not how the world works. Even if I wanted to live this way, if I actually gave to all who begged, I would soon not have anything to give because I would be reduced to being a beggar." A troubling problem, to be sure, but we at least need to remember that there is no indication in the Gospels that Jesus worked for a living. Surely, he was not a beggar. Yet, it is hard to avoid that unwelcome conclusion even in the land of Adam Smith. You must remember that from Smith's perspective, capitalism is the most charitable form of economic relation because no one in a capitalist world will have to beg. Yet, it seems that Jesus would not let us forget we are beggars.

Even more troubling, it seems we must turn the other cheek. The temptation, of course, is to read this as a clever strategy to put our enemies at a disadvantage. Surely, our enemy will not strike us again if it is clear we will not fight back. Yet, Jesus offers us no assurance that our enemy will not strike the other cheek. Loving our enemies is not a way to get what we want by more subtle strategies. Rather, we are required to love our enemies, to lend expecting nothing in return, because God is like that. If we so live, Jesus promises that our reward will be great because we will have become "children of the Most High; for he is kind to the ungrateful and the wicked. Be merciful, just as your Father is merciful."

That is a reminder that nonviolence is surely immoral if God is not the providential Lord of history, which means that Christians believe, as John Howard Yoder put it in *The Politics of Jesus*:

> The cross and not the sword, suffering and not brute power,

determines the meaning of history. The key to the obedience of God's people is not their effectiveness but their patience (Revelation 13:10). The triumph of the right is assured not by the might that comes to the aid of the right, which is of course the justification of the use of violence and other kinds of power in every human conflict; the triumph of the right, although it is assured, is sure because of the power of the resurrection and not because of any calculation of causes and effects, nor because of the inherently greater strength of the good guys. The relationship between the obedience of God's people and the triumph of God's cause is not a relationship of cause and effect but one of cross and resurrection. (232)

We do not know how God will use our faithfulness. We do not know how God's calling of Israel and the church will work out for the destiny of God's creation, but we do know we have seen God's providential care of us in the cross and resurrection of Christ. That is all we need to know, not only to live hopeful lives but to be God's hope for a world that otherwise has no basis for hope—for our hope entails that the wrongs of the past can be redeemed through forgiveness and reconciliation. What good news for us called to be God's people and what good news for a war torn world!

From Bennettsville, South Carolina to Scotland

Possessed by possessions, we have no idea what we ask when we pray to you, Beggar King, to free us from all that prevents us from praying to you as beggars. We work hard and believe we deserve what we make. Of course, the more we make and get what we deserve through our making, the lonelier lonely we become. Money is the way I can say I do not need anyone but myself. So, we learn to call our loneliness freedom. God knows that I am more than willing to give to the "deserving poor," but you surely do not mean to ask us, your good and decent people, to become poor. I am not clever or smart enough to survive in a world of money without money. So, make me, make us, capable of receiving gifts without regrets. I need to warn you, Jesus, to give me a soul capable of begging is not going to be easy.

Disrupting Time

Another week, another prayer, busy, busy, busy. How did I get myself into all this? It all just seems like work, but how can prayer be work? For prayer to be work surely means I have forgotten that I am praying to God. So, this prayer, the prayer before the lecture, just becomes part of the lecture. Jesus, you may have created us, but did you have to gift us with gifts that can make us so devious? I know I cannot make this prayer by trying harder. Trying harder just makes me more self-absorbed, which means that all I can do is ask you, Creator and Redeemer of all that is, to take this jumble of words and transform them, this class, and me into prayer.

From Bennettsville, South Carolina to Scotland

Lord of all life, we come before you not knowing who we are. We strut our stuff, trying to impress others with self-confidence. In the process, we hope to be what we pretend. Save us from such pretense, that we might learn who we are through trust in you to make us more than we can imagine. Help us, Augustine-like, to reread our lives as confessions of sin made possible by your love. Bind up our wounds and our joys so that our lives finally make sense only as a prayer to you. Amen.

Disrupting Time

Envy—surely, I am not envious. I have everything I want. We have wonderful lives. We say constantly, "Thank you, Lord, for the gift of your Son." How could a people so thankful be envious? Yet, I know I burn with envy. Life is just so unfair. Why should John or Mary be so damned smart and impressive and I have to work so hard just to get by? Of course, I can't let my envy show. Indeed, I cannot acknowledge how envy shapes my life even to myself. So, what are we to ask you to do, Abraham's God, about our envy? I really am not sure, but I think that nothing is more important than that you have given us good work to do. Consume our lives with your Spirit so that so consumed we may look up and say, "Thank God for Mary; thank God for John. I do not know what I would do without them." Amen.

Boasting in the Third Heaven
A Sermon Preached at Holy Family Episcopal
July 6, 2003

II Samuel 5: 1-5, 9-10
II Corinthians 12: 2-10
Mark 6: 1-13

I know a person in Christ who fourteen years ago was caught up to the third heaven—whether in the body or out of the body I do not know; God knows. And I know that such a person—whether in the body or out of the body I do not know; God knows—was caught up into Paradise and heard things that are not to be told, that no mortal is permitted to repeat. On behalf of such a one I will boast.

I was a student at Southwestern University in Georgetown, Texas from 1958-1962. There is a deep dispute between Southwestern and Baylor about which is the oldest school in Texas. Southwestern actually started earlier, but was put out of business for a few years by a cholera epidemic. That such a dispute exists gives you some idea that we are not talking about places (at least at the time I was in school) inhabited by highly sophisticated people. But, while I was at Southwestern, which is only twenty-six miles from Austin, I fell in love with the films of Ingmar Bergman. A theater in Austin often had Bergman film festivals.

Years later I was teaching at Augustana College in Rock Island, Illinois.

Augustana was a college of the Augustana Synod of the Swedish Lutheran Church. During my first year at Augustana I was reporting to a colleague how deeply I admired Bergman's films. What a world his imagination creates. The darkness, the landscape itself, seems to pulse with existential despair, the complexity of human relations so dramatically presented. My colleague was not impressed. He asked me if I had ever been to Sweden. I confessed that I had not. He said, "Well it's like that." "Oh!" I said. A valuable lesson learned.

I have even learned to make use of that lesson. When a foreigner, that is, someone who is not from the South, begins to tell me how much he or she admires the work of Flannery O'Connor, how he or she is drawn into the bizarre world she creates to depict this God haunted land, how he or she loves her gothic imagination, and so on and so on, I say, "Have you ever lived in the South? It's like that. If you have a good pickup truck with a gun rack on the back, you don't need Jesus."

> I know a person in Christ who fourteen years ago was caught up to the third heaven—whether in the body or out of the body I do not know; God knows. And I know that such a person—whether in the body or out of the body I do not know; God knows—was caught up into Paradise and heard things that are not to be told, that no mortal is permitted to repeat. On behalf of such a one I will boast.

Sweden is Sweden, the South is the South, but the "third heaven?" What are we to make of "third heaven"? It seems best to read over such passages quickly. Who among us is able to say, "It's like that"? We do not believe in third heavens, and we would distrust anyone who would report having been there. Paul seems to support our skepticism about third heavens by observing that those who have been there hear things they cannot repeat. Surely, talk about or belief in third heavens is not crucial to the Gospel.

Theologians have made careers trying to assure us that we do not have to believe in third heavens. In his famous book, *Jesus Christ and Mythology* (1958), Rudolf Bultmann observed that the conception of the world presupposed by the New Testament is mythological. That is, the world is structured in three stories, supernatural powers intervene in the course of events, miracles happen, and it is thought that we can be tempted and corrupted by the devil and evil spirits. According to Bultmann, however, modern people—people who flick light switches to turn on the lights—cannot believe in such a world (15). Our world is one of cause and effect, making it impossible for us to believe the myths constitutive of the Gospel.

Do not despair, gentle people. Bultmann has a solution. We can demythologize the Gospel. It turns out that Jesus was but an early representative of existentialism. Of course, we are told that Jesus was led into the wilderness to be tempted by the devil, but we know he actually confronted the existential nothingness of his existence and after going through sufficient angst made the decisive decision "to be." There, don't you feel better? Jesus does turn out to be a lot like us, a whole lot.

Of course, the problem with this strategy is that you begin not believing in "third heavens," and before you know it, you think that Jesus' resurrection is equally mythological. Those of us who are Protestants are particularly susceptible to this strategy because we have come to think that what makes Protestantism Protestantism is all the stuff we do not have to believe that the Catholics do believe. Protestants more or less have the attitude that they will only believe what makes sense to them. Catholics start with the attitude of, "Look at all the good stuff we get to believe!"

I am a Protestant, but I should like to be a Catholic. What, however, are we to do with "third heavens?" I think that we need to begin by noticing that Paul is not writing about our need to believe in third heavens. Paul is writing about boasting. He tells us that he will boast for the one who has been so caught up. To be caught up into Paradise is a sign of spiritual strength. To have something good happen to us can be a sign of God's favor. The tribes of Israel acknowledge David as their king, David occupies Jerusalem, and we are told, "David became greater and greater, for the Lord, the God of hosts, was with him." Of course, you have to be careful with greatness since it can be, as it was for David, a way to forget who you serve.

But, Paul tells us he would be a fool to boast in his strength. Rather, he will boast in his weakness. Now think about his refusal to boast in his strength. Saul saw Jesus on the Damascus road. Jesus spoke to Saul on the Damascus road. Saul's sight was restored by Ananias. Saul, now Paul, is counted among the apostles to be a witness to the gentiles. Indeed, Paul says to the Corinthians that "even considering the exceptional character of the revelations" he has been granted, he will not boast in them. Rather, he will boast in the thorn in his flesh that was given to him to stop him from being too elated.

Note that Paul is anything but happy about this "thorn." He says that he asked the Lord three times to take the thorn away, but instead he is told that "power is made perfect in weakness." So, Paul will "boast gladly in his weakness" so that Christ may dwell in him. He even says that he is content with "weaknesses, insults, hardships, persecutions, and calamities for the sake of Christ; for whenever I am weak, then I am strong." Indeed, in his letter to the Romans, Paul tells us, "The Spirit helps us in our weakness; for we do not know how to pray as we ought, but that very Spirit intercedes with sighs too deep for words."

I do not know how all this strikes you, but I have to tell you that I am very suspicious of Paul's appeal to weakness. I distrust people who make a life out of being weak. Too often, those who call attention to their weakness are trying to get us to do something we otherwise do not want to do. It is enough to make you want to return to the questions about third heavens. Indeed, I suspect that one of the reasons we feel we need to demythologize the New Testament is we think third heavens are for the weak. But we, that is, people who know how to take care of ourselves, do not need comforting myths to get through life. All we need is to "believe in ourselves," or some other equally lame platitude we use to assure ourselves that we are all right.

Think about, for example, what we have just done, that is, celebrated the Fourth of July. How many times did you hear that we should be grateful to live in the greatest and strongest nation in the history of the world? If it is true that America is the greatest nation, it seems from Paul's point of view that is not necessarily good news. From Paul's perspective, it seems that we might be better off if we lost the war against terrorism.

Well, maybe Paul did not mean to imply that his boasting in weakness applied to nations and empires, but I suspect that we are equally unhappy to think that Paul's boasting in weakness might apply to our everyday lives. For example, consider how we think about being sick. We usually think that it is perfectly all right to be sick for a while. We even think when we are sick that we can demand special attention and care, but we also know that we can do so only if we are trying to get well. Do we really want people among us who boast in their disability because they believe God has blessed them by making them sick? Do we want to say with the Orthodox monk, Ioannikios, "For one to be ill is a divine visitation. Illness is the greatest gift from God. The only thing that man can give to God is pain."

Think how such a view of illness would transform our understanding of medicine. For example, Basil the Great (329-379) observed that the medical arts were given to us to relieve the sick. Christians, therefore, can be called to the office of medicine because we believe that medical interventions are appropriate as long as they do not impede the spiritual life. However, St. Basil warns that we should avoid "whatever requires an undue amount of thought or trouble or involves a large expenditure of effort and causes our whole life to revolve, as it were, around the solicitude for the flesh." Is it possible for us to believe that our frailties, our becoming sick, may actually be a way that Christ's power is made perfect in and through us?

When I lived in South Bend, Indiana, I was a member of Broadway United Methodist Church. The church was in a poor section of South Bend, but that meant some good things were possible because we had nothing to lose. For example, after long study and prayer we moved to every Sunday Eucharist. By sharing in Christ's meal, we were led to prepare a meal after church every Sunday for the neighborhood, inviting anyone who wanted to come. Many street people came to the meal, but they seldom joined in our worship. However, one bag lady began to show up every Sunday to join us for our ten o'clock worship service. We were largely a congregation of white liberals who came to church to assure one another we did not need one another. Not this bag lady. Long schooled on the prayers of the African-American church, she would pray, "Dear Lord, I am hurting this week. I have a cold and my legs hurt. Make these people help me." A Paul had come amongst us. We did not know quite what to make of the fact that she was with us, but we began to discover that during the prayers of the church we too could ask for help.

Let me be very clear. I am not suggesting nor do I think that Paul is suggesting that Christians are to rush out and try to be weak. That would be another way to try to be strong. Paul does not boast in his weakness because being weak is a good in and of itself, but because in some small fashion our weakness can witness to the One who refuses to redeem the world through violence. Jesus not being honored among his own—indeed we are told that he could do no deed of power there—is a reminder that God refuses to storm the walls of our rebellion on our terms. Through the Son the Father is subjected to the worst we can do, yet God triumphs through, of all things, a cross. The cross is not some manipulative strategy for God to be able to get what God wants by making us feel guilty. Rather, the cross witnesses that God's very being is a love that has all the time in the world to endure patiently our frightened and prideful refusal to worship a crucified savior. Can we really bring ourselves to believe that our weakness could be the occasion where we too learn, even as Americans, to suffer, and through suffering to endure, and by enduring to triumph?

We are talking, of course, about a miracle, for we believe that every Sunday God can do and does, even here among people like us, a deed of great power. The power of the deed, however, continues to have the form of crucifixion. So, Sunday after Sunday, bread and wine is made for us the body and blood of Christ. The bread and wine being so made means, as we pray after Eucharist, that we who receive the body and blood become "living members of your Son our Savior Jesus Christ." Whatever it may mean to be "caught up to the third heaven," it will not mean more than what it means for us to be made living members of our Savior Jesus Christ. So, if asked what you make of "third heavens," point to what God will do for us and with us in this Eucharist and say, "This is that."

From Bennettsville, South Carolina to Scotland

You have commanded us to be a people of prayer. That seems a little extreme. Would not it have been a better strategy to make us creatures that want to pray? Why command when you can want us to want you? Yet, I confess most of the time I do not want to pray. Indeed, most of the time, I do not even know how to pray or to whom I am praying. Maybe being commanded to pray is not a bad idea. So, I pray that you will help us discover that your commands are life-giving, making us a people who desire to pray because we have learned to pray through your command.

The Good Samaritan: An Expository Sermon

Psalm 25
Deuteronomy 30: 9-14
Colossians 1: 1-14
Luke 10: 25-37

The story of the Good Samaritan has not been a good story for Christians, particularly in this time called modern. We, of course, love this story. This story reinforces our assumption that whatever it may mean to be a Christian, it at least means we ought to care for the needy neighbor. We assume that we are or should be "Samaritans," outsiders, gentiles who care for the neighbor in defiance of a law-determined ethic or religious dogma. Such care we call loving.

That we think the story of the Good Samaritan is about love is quite reasonable. When queried by Jesus concerning what is written in the law, the lawyer answered with what we now know as the great commandment: "You shall love the Lord your God with all your heart, and with all your soul, and with all your strength, and with all your mind; and your neighbor as yourself." So, love seems to be what Jesus is about, and the story of the Samaritan is the exemplification of such love.

I have to tell you that I think the identification of Christianity with love has been one of the reasons we have so much trouble understanding why we are Christians in our day. If we are all in agreement that we ought to love one another, why do we need Jesus to tell us that? If Jesus is really all about love, if Jesus' ministry can be summed up by the claim, "When all is said and done we ought to love one another," then why did he have to die? That he was put to death must have been the result of a terrible failure in communication. Why would you put to death someone who is recommending that we love one another?

This emphasis on love as what "Christianity is all about," I fear, has had a more deleterious result. To make Christianity all about love tempts us to underwrite what I can only call a "silent anti-semitism." The anti-semitism is silent because we assume that as people who are taught to love everybody we also ought to love the Jews. However, notice how the story of the Good Samaritan works. The priest and the Levite, whom we assume were Jews, pass by the beaten man, but the Samaritan—one of those despised by the Jews for their non-recognition of the centrality of the temple—takes the time to care for the man who fell among thieves. The sub-text is unmistakable: Jews think it more important to keep the law than to act from love. That is, moreover, what makes Christians Christians and Jews Jews. The Jews are people of the law but Christians think that love trumps any law.

I think, therefore, that it is very important to read our texts for today closely, because when we do so, the love story we assume is the story of the Good Samaritan turns out to be a good deal more complex. Why, for example, does the lawyer suddenly feel it important to test Jesus? What does it mean to be a "lawyer?" We, that is, those of us who are not biblical scholars, assume that we have to wait for the historians to answer these questions. I certainly would not want to denigrate the importance of historical scholarship. For example, that we now understand that the Pharisees and Jesus shared far more than they differed, we owe to the work of scholars such as W.D. Davies. However, I think that there is quite enough in the text itself to help us answer these questions.

Lawyers, it turns out, were a lot like Pharisees. In chapter eleven of the book of Luke, Jesus denounces the Pharisees for keeping the laws surrounding food, for being concerned with minutiae, for desiring to be honored, and yet lacking the virtues of love and justice that the law requires. One of the lawyers responded by noting that when Jesus gored the Pharisees' ox he was also insulting the lawyers. The lawyers, it seems, were the scholars of the law committed to helping Israel remember that the law, the whole law, was her salvation. The lawyers and the Pharisees assumed, as we are told in Deuteronomy, that "to turn to the Lord your God with all your heart and with all your soul," meant that Israel would desire to "obey the Lord your God by observing his commandments and decrees that are written in this book of the law." Such obedience, moreover, was the way the Pharisees and the lawyers resisted the loss of identity that is always a threat to a people who are ruled by an occupying power. Unable to resist the Romans by violence, the Pharisees and the lawyers were determined to resist by living lives of holiness.

It is, therefore, quite interesting that the lawyer in our text for today felt the need to "test Jesus." He did so, I think, because our text follows from Jesus' sending of the seventy, who returned reporting, "Even the demons submitted to us." Jesus admonished them not to get too carried away with their newfound power, but Jesus also took this as an opportunity to thank the Father for hiding "these things" from the wise and intelligent, but revealing it to infants. What has been revealed, Jesus tells us, is that all things have been "handed over to me by my Father; and no one knows who the Son is except the Father, or who the Father is except the Son and anyone to whom the Son chooses to reveal him" (Luke 10: 22). Jesus, then, in private tells that ragtag group of dunderheads whom we call the disciples that kings have desired to see and hear what they now see and hear. It turns out that to be powerful, to be rich, does not position us well to know who this Jesus is.

So, we should not be surprised that the lawyer felt the need to test Jesus. This guy is a university professor of Christian ethics, and he suddenly feels threatened by this Jesus who says that the uneducated know more than he knows. So, he asks what he must do to inherit eternal life, that is, to be saved. Jesus responds by playing to the lawyer's strength: "What is written in the law? What do you read there?" Notice that Jesus' response assumes that the law is about salvation. The lawyer, moreover, proves astute, conjoining Deuteronomy 5:6 and Leviticus 19:18 to link love of God to love of neighbor.

In Matthew 22 and Mark 12 Jesus responds to those who test him by giving the great commandment, but in Luke the lawyer speaks the great commandment. This is very interesting because there is a scholarly debate concerning whether the commandment, whether these two verses from different books, had been conjoined in Judaism prior to their being conjoined in the Gospels. Some people doubt that such a summary could be Jewish, particularly if the great commandment was assumed to replace all 613 commandments of the law. However, in Luke it is clear that at least one Jew, this lawyer, knows the great commandment. Jesus responds, saying that he has given the right answer, and if he does what the commandment asks he "will live," that is, he will know salvation.

Then, we are told that the lawyer, "wanting to justify himself," asks, "And who is my neighbor?" This is very curious. He gave the right answer. Why does he feel a need to "justify himself"? Jesus' response, "Do this, and you will live," seems to challenge the lawyer in a way he had not expected. The lawyer had begun wanting to discuss a nice point of the law, but it turns out that Jesus is not an academic. Jesus is deadly serious—"Do this and you will live."

At this point Christians are tempted to use this text to celebrate that we understand something this lawyer, who we believe represents the Jews, just does not get. It is all about love. However, that response fails to account for Jesus' answer to "a certain ruler" (Luke 18:18) who also asked him, "Good Teacher, what must I do to inherit eternal life?" Jesus said to him, "Why do you call me good? No one is good but God alone. You know the commandments: 'You shall not commit adultery; you shall not murder; you shall not steal; you shall not bear false witness; honor your father and mother.'" The questioner of Jesus answers that he has kept all these commandments only to be told by Jesus that he should sell all he has and give it to the poor. After he has done so, Jesus commands him, "Then come, follow me." Hearing this, the man went away sad because he was very rich.

Law is not the problem. Love is not the problem. The relation between love and law is not the problem. The problem is, "Then come, follow me." The problem quite simply is Jesus. The lawyer who stood up to test Jesus rightly understood that Jesus is a teacher, but he did not understand that this teacher is the One capable of revealing the Father. The Father has handed all things over to Jesus, making all things new. To know the great commandment, to know the precepts of the law, to know what love entails requires that we must know how to follow this One. If you want to know what all 613 commandments require, follow Jesus. If you want to know what love is, follow Jesus.

Disrupting Time

In Colossians Paul tells us that God has "rescued us from the power of darkness and transferred us into the kingdom of his beloved Son, in whom we have redemption, the forgiveness of sins." Because we have been so rescued, Paul prays for the Colossians and for us that we may be filled with spiritual wisdom and understanding and therefore be capable of leading "lives worthy of the Lord, fully pleasing to him as you bear fruit in every good work and as you grow in the knowledge of God." It is about holiness. It is about resisting the occupying powers. But, that resistance takes the form of a Samaritan's refusal to pass by the neighbor who has been robbed and beaten. Jesus has given us the time in an unjust world to take the time to care for the neighbor one neighbor at a time.

In our time, a time given by God, I believe that Christians are being forced to discover that whatever we are, we will not be faithful if we pridefully think that we are different from Jews. Israel has been forced, time and time again, to learn how to wait. We believe that Jesus has made the waiting that is the church, the waiting taught by the law, our love-shaped waiting, into eternal life. Our confidence that through Jesus' birth, life, death, and resurrection the world has been redeemed makes it possible for us to be a patient, waiting, holy people.

Paul hopes that the Colossians may "be made strong with all the strength that comes from his glorious power, and may you be prepared to endure everything with patience, while joyfully giving thanks to the Father, who has enabled you to share in the inheritance of the saints in the light." If we are to be what we have been made, let us pray that God makes us patient, capable of not only knowing the great commandment but also being for our neighbors and ourselves the love unleashed by the Father's love of the Son made ours through the Spirit.

I suspect that many of you find, as I do, the language of holiness too grand to describe the lives we live, but Paul says we share in the inheritance of the saints. Indeed, after the Eucharist we will pray, "Eternal God, heavenly Father, you have graciously accepted us as living members of your Son our Savior Jesus Christ." "Living members of the Son"—that is what it means to be holy, to receive and to be made the body and the blood. Moreover, when a eucharistic minister is given the elements to take to those unable to be with us due to sickness or age, we become Samaritans for one another and for the world. And, Jesus says to us, "Go

From Bennettsville, South Carolina to Scotland

and do likewise." So doing, we discover that though from time to time we may be called to be Samaritans, most of the time, and particularly at this table, we are those who were beaten and left to die, for whom God takes the time in this meal to bind up our wounds, and in so binding them heals the world.

Disrupting Time

"You made us for yourself and our hearts are restless until they rest in you." So Augustine begins his *Confessions*. Is restless just another word for love? If so, Augustine is surely right that we have such difficulty getting our loves right. We find that we cannot even rightly love ourselves. We cannot because we think we know ourselves all too well. But, of course, our presumption of knowledge even of ourselves is part of the problem. Only when we know, only when we love, as you know and love us, do we know ourselves. But, from where does such knowledge come? Surely, it is as close as the neighbor next to whom we sit. So, thank you for giving us neighbors, the strangest being ourselves.

Sermons on the Occasion of Marriage

How the Virgin Birth Makes Marriage Possible

Song of Solomon 2: 8-13
Psalm 89: 1-18
Luke 1: 26-38

Three days before Christmas is an unlikely time for a wedding. We are still in Advent. Advent is a time of waiting. Advent does not sound like a wedding. Advent suggests an extended engagement. Only secular people get married before Christmas, and they usually live in California, that place where not only the Christian year is unknown, but time itself does not exist. So, what in the world are Demery and Scott, who are decidedly not secular—at least less secular than most of us—doing getting married at this time? This wedding is obviously a prophetic sign-act. If only we could figure out what the sign signifies.

The joy that Demery and Scott's marriage occasions is sufficient reason for most of us to forgive them for subjecting us to a wedding during Advent. This is particularly true for Paula and me. We cannot help but see a bit of ourselves in Scott and Demery. That is, I am like Scott, a layman and a bit older, marrying someone who is first and foremost a minister. Yet, there is one significant difference between us as couples, which makes me worry about this marriage. I am referring, of course, to the fact that Paula and I are Methodists while Scott and Demery are in the Reformed tradition.

Paula and I are confident that we are being made perfect. Calvinists know they *are* the elected. In marriage, I have to think, becoming is better than being. "Being elected" always makes one so unsure whether the others who claim to be elected really are. So, election becomes a source of conflict, and marriage usually has enough potential sources of conflict without adding election. Moreover, we have a UCC marrying a Presbyterian. Can Demery be confident that Scott will ever believe a church can be the church without elders? No matter how confessional Demery may be, will Scott ever believe that you can be the church without the Westminster confession? Dramatic stuff. I can see the *National Enquirer* headlines now: "Theologian asks wife as a reaffirmation of their love to say the Westminster confession—backwards."

You can see that for this marriage to work they are going to need a lot of help. Of course, that is why we are here: to pledge our help. Yet, our help, no matter how good-willed, would be futile if we were just another human community. But, we are not just another human community. We are the church of Jesus Christ. That is, we are those people created by the Virgin Mary's, "Here am I, the servant of the Lord; let it be with me according to your word." Without the miracle of the virgin birth, the hope constituted by this marriage could not help but be false and futile.

An unlikely time to be married, an unlikely text—the Annunciation—to have for a marriage. When I first began to think about this sermon, and about what Demery and Scott had done by asking me to preach on the lectionary texts, I kept thinking, "If I am to be true to the text I ought to start with an announcement: Scott, old buddy, I have some astounding news—you are pregnant, and Demery is going to take care of you anyway." Not a bad way for us to begin, if we are to have some slight appreciation of what it meant for Mary to say, "Here am I."

Yet, this unlikely time and text are just right for us to remember what God does here. This is a Christian marriage. Scott and Demery are going to make unconditional promises to one another. We are going to hold them to those promises, and those promises, thus, become constitutive of our lives. Put differently, what we do here is not simply a reflection of community; it is how we become the community made possible by the virgin birth. By pledging to be faithful to one another for a lifetime, Demery and Scott make us timeful people, capable of sharing one another's stories. As David McCarthy, a former graduate student (yes, Mrs. Saye [mother of Scott], they really do graduate) put it to me recently, "Have you ever considered what it would do to the rest of our lives if your and Paula's marriage went bust?" I cannot remember if Scott or Demery know David and Bridget, but I know that their stories are now part of one another's.

That might make any of us think, "Is this something we want to get into? I am not sure I wanted this many people in my life. We just thought we were getting married. Isn't marriage a legitimation of a couple's mutual narcissism? Now you tell us that when we make these promises to one another, we become part of a web of stories we have not chosen. Maybe we should rethink this." If Scott and Demery are tempted to think these thoughts, we can say, "Too late! By God, if you got us here during Advent, we are surely going to make you go through with this."

Of course, much more important than whatever is going on in Scott's or Demery's or any of our subjectivities is the question of what gives them or us the presumption that we can make such promises? Surely, such promises are presumptive if Mary is not the virgin mother of our Lord Jesus Christ. The hope and the patience made possible by the child Mary conceived, the same hope and patience that constitute time itself, particularly that time called Advent, make marriage possible. Marriage, life-long fidelity, only makes sense as part of the new age begun in this virgin's "Here am I."

For us, that is, us moderns, the virgin birth is often used as a test case for how far we are willing to go in believing what most people think is unbelievable. Yet, what could be more believable than for the God praised in Psalm 89 to come to us in a virgin's womb. For this God, whose love is as true and firm as the ancient earth and whose faithfulness is as fixed as the heavens, this God alone is able to be nearer to us than we can be to ourselves. This God, and this God alone, provides us with the confidence to make our loves marriage.

"The Holy One of Israel, He is our King." The Holy One of Israel alone is strong enough to gently redeem through a virgin's faithfulness. Through this virgin, our mother, we are grafted into Israel, made part of God's very life, so that the world may know that we have the time to rest easy, to enjoy, God's good creation. We even have the time to be married, confident that God would not have God's kingdom come through impatient violence. After all, the redemption found in the virgin's belly is the redemption of creation. Even marriage, one of the given gifts of creation, is now redeemed for service in God's kingdom.

In our time marriage has become for some, far too many I fear, a desperate act against the loneliness we fear threatens to engulf us. Marriage becomes a substitute for community in a society bent on denying time rather than the couple's drawing on the habits of a timeful community. The lusty love of the Song of Solomon, which, I am sure Demery and Scott would want me to remind you, is first and foremost an account of Christ's love for his church, becomes in our time fearful. In modern time, which is but a way of saying all that time that is not advent, the love of the beloved is so precious we cannot enjoy the having of it. The very time such love creates becomes a threat since it cannot help but suggest loss, for our loves beacon our death, and we do not know how to love in the face of death.

Thank God that is not the marriage or the love we celebrate in this time of Advent—a time no longer determined by fear of death, conquered as death was by this babe's cross. Thank God for Demery and Scott who say to God, to us, and to one another, "Here am I." Thank God we know that this is a marriage made possible by the love God unleashed on the world through a virgin birth. Thank God that they share their love with us, knowing that in that sharing is the courage necessary for us to have the patience to give to one another the gift of constancy. Thank God that, on this eve of the incarnation of our Lord, Scott and Demery have given us this time to celebrate their marriage. What a hopeful thing to do at Advent.

An Apocalyptic Marriage

Revelation 19: 4-10
I Corinthians 13
John 3: 16-18

What the church is about to do to you is a fearful thing. We are to witness God's declaration that you are to be married to one another for life. The vows you will make to one another are frightening enough, but these vows indicate that this act, this marriage, is an action of the end times. Apocalyptic, that is, God's final revealing of what remains hidden, does not just name the unexpected—events, for example, as surprising as Bill's discovery that he loves Joan more than fishing. Rather, apocalyptic names the time required to give you the patience you will need to discover the love that makes marriage, and in particular, your marriage, a sign that God's rule is a present reality.

We, the church, understand that you love one another, but we are not particularly impressed by that fact. It is a start. For, as A. S. Byatt observes, falling in love is "a kind of storytelling that makes you coherent." Partners in love discover, are enthralled by, the possibilities that come from finding that they are not only physically desirable to one another, but that they share a solidarity and complexity that requires as well as gives them time to explore what they have been given, that is, time to share a story. Rowan Williams, a theologian who happens to be the Archbishop of Canterbury, describes the discovery that we are loved and love another as a promise. Such a promise takes the form of countless small actions and details through which I learn who I am from another in a manner I could never have learned by myself. In short, love names the exhilaration I experience from the recognition that I am interesting to another human being.

Yet, the Archbishop observes that this discovery is fraught with ambiguity. Being in love intensifies my sense of being me, but that very intensification requires a confrontation with what is absolutely not me. Therefore, being in love "hovers between egotism and self-denial." Because I know my lover will discover my mediocrity or destructiveness, I seek ways to mold and control the interest of the one I love. I become afraid to speak the truth, not because I am a liar, but because I fear losing what the one I have come to love has given me. We never lie to those we love or to ourselves more readily than when we lie in service of the intimacy we have achieved based on half-truths. The conviction that there is room for me in another's life at once invites me to be more than I am and to a self-effacement born of the fear that I will lose myself if I lose the other.

The power the other has over my life that love so often names takes the form of a history shaped by the habits of the everyday. We may repress the fears that lurk in love in the busy forgetfulness of making wedding plans, moving to a new place, negotiating one another's families, making new friends, and most of all, learning to get by on a reduced income. Such is the stuff that makes up the story that love not only makes possible, but also requires. Yet, the story that becomes the way we express our love for one another threatens to domesticate the danger that must remain if our love for one another is to be truthful. So, marriages are always risky business.

This brings us to the good news that God's love reconstitutes our love of one another by the story, by the time, which makes it possible for Christians to give themselves to one another in marriage. Christians can risk marriage, not because we love one another, but because God risked his Son so that we might be capable of loving our enemies—enemies, moreover, who often turn out to be our husbands, our wives, and most of all, ourselves. A love capable of loving enemies is not, as Christians often presume, God's willingness to accept us without conditions. In a loveless world, or a world of misshapen loves, it is understandable that many want God to be the lover of last resort. When no one else loves us, at least we think God loves us. Yet, God's love is not a love of generalized acceptance.

God's love is this Jesus whose resurrection has inaugurated a new age and a new people.

> "Hallelujah!
> For the Lord our God
>   the Almighty reigns.
> Let us rejoice and exult
>   and give him the glory,
> for the marriage of the Lamb has come,
>   and his bride has made herself ready;
> to her it has been granted to be clothed
>   with fine linen, bright and pure" –

The "bride who has made herself ready" is we, the church. We are the people of the new age clothed in the fine linen of our baptisms. The love that is the love of God is now to be found in this people who have been made worthy by God to be the bride of the lamb. What was once a hope has become a reality. The world is no longer forced to live by the stories of the world's distorted loves that ultimately require us to kill or be killed. The world has been restoried—and thus, restored—by the love of God found in this savior, Jesus Christ, and by his people, the church of Jesus Christ. We are the people of the end time capable of dying and, thus, of living in a manner that the world may know that there is an alternative to the deathly loves of the world.

Such a people are capable of living in the world without being "of it." They are capable of making promises to one another, which, if Jesus has not been raised from the dead, could not help but appear foolish. "Until we are parted by death." Really! Could people really "know" what they are promising when they say they will be faithful to another "until they are parted by death"? Of course, Joan and Bill cannot know what they are promising when they make that promise to God, to us, and to one another. That they are able to make such a promise is because through their baptisms they are already part of God's promise that makes their promise of fidelity to one another intelligible.

This means that the story Joan and Bill's love has begun through their marriage is but part of the story of God's love for God's church. If that love, God's love, does not animate God's people, then what we do here cannot help but be a disaster. As much as we delight in your love of one another, we must remember that your love is not "yours," but through marriage is made part of God's care for us in the church. The patience, the kindness, that love is, the love that is neither irritable or resentful, that love is not envious, boastful, arrogant or rude; that love rejoices in truth—these are not recommendations for the kind of love necessary to have a "happy" marriage. Rather, Paul's great hymn of love describes the love that animates the body of Christ, the church, made present through the inauguration of the new age.

That is why this marriage, indeed all our marriages, must be celebrated, must be storied, eucharistically. "Blessed are those who are invited to the marriage supper of the Lamb." This is the feast of the new age that makes this marriage not only possible, but also a witness to the reality of God's reign. Here we discover that love is not a scarce resource to be hoarded for fear that it will be used up. Through this meal, we discover, time and time again, that God has held nothing in reserve, giving all so that we may be gifts for one another. That is why this marriage is such good news. In a world as dark as ours you have been called to be married.

How extraordinary! How wonderful! Thanks be to God. Amen.

Rightly Dressed
For August 10, 2002

Isaiah 61:10-62:3
Revelation 15:9-17
John 15:9-17

Stuart Henry, that small ball of Calvinist wisdom who was predestined to live out his years among the obsessively optimistic Methodists at the Divinity School at Duke, knew a great deal about marriage. He knew a great deal about marriage because he had never been married. Accordingly, he watched and learned. One of the things he knew was that one should never give advice to those about to be married. They are hopelessly filled with the hope of fresh love, making it impossible for them to hear the extraordinary promises they are going to make to one another. Limited people making unlimited promises might make one stop and think but, as Stuart knew, even committed Calvinists persist in getting married.

However, Stuart did favor me with an observation close to the wedding that would join Paula and me in marriage. He told me not to worry about how I might look at our wedding because no one would be looking at me. Paula would be the object of attention. All eyes would be on her. According to Stuart, the groom exists only because you have to have a groom in order for there to be a bride. Even though I thought that I looked pretty good in a tux, I took solace in Stuart's observation. I could relax and enjoy our wedding, secure in the knowledge that I was not going to be the center of attention.

Stuart's observation, I suspect, also applies to the role of sermons in marriage liturgies. Liturgies for the solemnization of marriage require a sermon, but who in their right mind (and those getting married are clearly not in their "right minds") is going to remember a wedding sermon? Remembering a wedding sermon would be as odd as remembering any commencement address at any academic level. Those to be praised or given advice are not in any mood to be told what a wonderful thing they have done or how they are to live now that they have done such a great thing. Praising or advising at a wedding seems even more futile than commencement orations.

Of course, this is a very strange marriage. Two Methodist ministers are to be married to one another. One is even doing doctoral work in the hope he may be able to help the church better understand what we do or should do when we preach. How would you like to be Ginger, knowing you are marrying someone who thinks not only that he should be an ongoing critic of preaching, but in particular of her preaching? This is clearly not a marriage made in heaven. Rather, this is clearly a marriage made in a divinity school.

My strategy when asked to preach at weddings is to avoid giving any advice to those being married. Rather, I try to remind them that neither the groom nor the bride is the center of attention. God is the center of attention even at a wedding. Accordingly, the crucial actor in this service is not those getting married, but the church that witnesses this marriage. Thus, the heavy responsibility on us who witness the vows Ginger and Roger make to one another is to hold them to those vows. For, the love they promise to one another is not a love peculiar to marriage, but is the love Christians have learned through the sharing of the body and blood of Christ. Thus, my oft made claim that one of the hardest commandments (and note that in the Gospel of John Jesus commands us to love one another) is that Christians are to love one another—even if they are married.

The texts that Roger and Ginger have chosen, however, have made me rethink my wedding-sermon strategy. I think I am right to call attention to the responsibility of those who witness their marriage, but these texts make clear that Ginger and Roger have responsibilities to us and God. It is interesting, moreover, that such responsibilities have to do with how they are dressed. Our scriptures for today call attention to the widespread desire to dress up for a wedding. Thus, in Isaiah we are told that the garments of salvation will cover us in a manner that a groom is garlanded and a bride is adorned with jewels. The book of Revelation, no doubt written by a Calvinist, directs our attention only to the bride who is clothed in bright and pure fine linen.

That bride, of course, is the church, but I think it a mistake, as I have done in the past wedding sermons, to focus only on what the church must be in order to make the vows Ginger and Roger make to one another intelligible. If we did not know something about brides (and perhaps even grooms) prior to our being the church, we would not know why it is so important for our understanding of the church that weddings are such celebratory events marked by the dress of those being married. The sheer joy that Roger and Ginger manifest in their discovery of one another, the enjoyment that their joy gives all of us gathered here, should tell us something about Christ's love of His church.

In Revelation John explicitly tells us that the fine linen, bright and pure, is "the righteous deeds of the saints." Phrases such as "the righteous deeds of the saints" are sufficiently unspecified to tempt us to speculate about how Ginger and Roger's love of one another may or may not count as such a deed. Yet, the scripture does not invite us to engage in that kind of speculation. Rather, we have the words of Jesus, which are all too clear about the nature of such deeds. The righteous deeds of the saints are formed by the love made possible by Jesus' love of us. Moreover, we are not left in the dark about such love: "No one has greater love than this, to lay down one's life for one's friends." If love just is laying down our lives for our friends, we can begin to understand why Jesus commands us to so love, rather than simply recommending that we do so.

Is the willingness to make such sacrifice the bright and pure linen that confirms the celebratory nature of this wedding and marriage? Surely not. Of course, Ginger and Roger will learn along the way that they will have to make yet unimagined sacrifices during the course of their marriage. We all know that marriage entails some sacrifice. For example, one of the hardest things we have to learn is that after an evening together there is no place to go. I cannot return to my apartment for some rest from the work of constant interaction. I am already at home, and I have no place to which I might escape. To be sure, the slow recognition that the person we married is not going to go away may be a school that slowly pulls us away from our self-centeredness, but such "sacrifices" are not sufficient to deserve the description of "laying down one's life."

Indeed, I think the language of "self-sacrifice" is dangerous when associated with marriage. In the past when self-sacrifice was recommended to sustain marriage, the recommendation was too often primarily directed at women and associated with the having of children. No doubt, few relations teach us more about our self-centeredness than the having of children, but—as children are quick to remind us—the sacrifices we make for their welfare can too often be turned into emotional blackmail. Even without children, self-sacrifice in marriage too easily becomes a power game in which I get to have my way because I have sacrificed more than my spouse has sacrificed. God, we are clever, devious, sinful creatures. Where is Stuart Henry when we really need him?

That is but a reminder that the marriage we celebrate between Ginger and Roger is not just another marriage. What we celebrate is a Christian marriage between Christians. The One who has the right to claim us as friends, so that we may be made friends of one another, makes such a marriage possible. Because of Christ's sacrifice for us, Roger and Ginger do not need to be married. They have all the friends they will need to negotiate this life of loneliness without being left alone. So, they do not marry because they are desperate to find a hedge against the darkness of isolation, but rather their marriage—like all marriages between Christians—witnesses the exuberance, the sheer wonder, in knowing that they are loved and thus can love one another.

So, by God, let us celebrate the wonderful thing Ginger and Roger do here for us. This marriage is gospel. In his wonderful book, *God and the New Haven Railway and Why Neither One Is Doing Very Well*, Dennis O'Brien observes:

> The muddle of loving is what traditional theologians call the problem of salvation. How can we give over our fate, happiness, and autobiographical rights to anyone else? This is *my* story. If I am obsessed with *my* story in the fashion of the self-help books, then salvation is distasteful because salvation *comes from another*.

In the older language it was "grace," a gift, something gratuitous. If the modern world seems particularly deaf to hymn singing, it may be because we are so convinced that the only story worth telling is self-scripted.

Roger and Ginger, baptized Christians, know that the only story capable of making their lives worthy is the one given to them by God. Accordingly, Roger and Ginger are the hymn, made possible by Christ's gift of himself, that defies the darkness by teaching us to trust our fleshy love of one another. By giving their lives to one another, they are made one by the God who has storied us through Jesus Christ and the Spirit. It, therefore, gives us great pleasure to say to Ginger and Roger, "Amen and Amen. What a wonderful thing you do for us."

Disrupting Time

Against the darkness of our lives, against the violence that threatens to overwhelm us, against the lies that make it impossible to know what is and is not true, against the dark cloak of cynicism we wear in the false hope that believing in no one or nothing we will be free from the lies, you give us children. How extraordinary, how simple that people as confused and lost as we are can still choose life. Amazing. So, I rejoice in the birth of Kendall Boynton Hauerwas. Make his life true and good. Delight him with the beauty of pine trees and wonder of cats—and, God help him, may he even come to understand the place of squirrels in your creation. So delighted, may he be pulled into your peaceful kingdom, and please, dear Jesus, may we be your peace for him.

Sermons on the Occasion of Marriage

Loving Lord, You have created us to be your lovers. The intensity of love scares us. Love threatens loss of self, loss of control, lostness amid the blackness of the cosmos. Against the blackness, we lunge for one another, hoping that our clinging to another can block out the meaninglessness of our lives. The intense beauty of such love, however, fades, doomed by the desperation of its birth. So, teach us to be truthful lovers. Help us desire You so that all our loves can delight in the sheer existence of that which we love. Help us remember that true love creates distance the closer such love draws us to that we love [H. Richard Niebuhr]. Order our loves so that we may rightly love grass, trees, bears, dogs, cats, and one another with your fear-free love. Help us see the "eaches" of your creation as witnesses of your love. So drawn to the beauty of your world, may our lives shine with the bright desire of your love so that we may even come to love ourselves.

Disrupting Time

Dear God, your church is being torn apart over questions of sex. How did we get to this place? What do we do now that we are at this place? It now seems necessary to take sides, but the sides require a confidence I cannot pretend to have. Help us learn to know how to have an argument. Help us learn how to live from one another. Help us learn how to go on when we are unclear whether there is a way forward. Help us not lose the love inspired by your Spirit. At the very least, save us from silliness that comes from trying to speak when we have nothing to say. Compel us to be united in service to your Son, and being so united, may the world say, "Those people love one another enough to have an argument."

Children, Father God, give us children. Give us those balls of energy that mess up and confuse our lives. Give us the unrelenting need children are, so that we are pulled into a world of love otherwise unimagined. Give us the story time children require, so that we might be restored by their love of us. Help us love these strange creatures in a manner that our love of this child does not tempt us to kill other children so that the children we love be safe. Help us remember that you would not have us love even our children with a love undisciplined by the love you have shown us in the crucifixion of your Son. So cared for, may the sheer exuberance of children make us joyful just to the extent that we learn that the patience children teach us is your Kingdom.

Disrupting Time

Dear God, we are surrounded by death. Death in Israel, death in Afghanistan, death in Iraq, death in America. America, we are told, is at war. It must be true because patriotism reigns. Help us remember that patriotism is easy. War is hard death. For what do we pray? For what do we hope? We feel so lost that we do not know what words to use, but suddenly there is hope. Tahlia is born. A baby whose hunger calls us to life, calls us to joy, calls us to love. A miracle, making a world possible that we had not the patience to imagine. Make this child a lover of you and the peace made real in Jesus' cross and resurrection. May she signal that the hope she is, is alternative to death. So, dear God, we thank you, we praise you, that in this time of death you have us hope that even we, your miserable creatures, can rejoice in the birth of a child.

Sermons on the Occasion of Marriage

Lustily you love us, Mary-born Lord. Embodied, you would not have us be etherealized spirits. Rather, we find that we are bodies all the way down. But, are our bodies the picture of the soul? That you have taken on our flesh surely entails that whatever more we may be, the "more" is not more than our bodies. But, our bodies beacon death . . . and love. Without bodies, we could not desire one another or you, but those same bodies become pain-filled and wrinkled. How extraordinary! I am growing old. In fact, I may already be old. I somehow had not noticed. Save me from the silliness, the body-denying silliness, to which the old are tempted. Help me, help us, behold bodily friends across generations, so that we might be for the world confident lovers who can say, "Until death do us part."

Callings:
The Ministry and Other Offices

For the Love of the Ministry

Deuteronomy 34: 1-12
Psalms 90: 1-6, 13-17
I Thessalonians 2: 1-8
Matthew 22: 34-46

    I confess that I feel a bit strange preaching to you on this occasion. Of course, I am honored to be here to celebrate Kyle's ten years as your pastor. That people like Kyle claim me for a friend makes my life possible. Strange creatures that we are, theologians are unintelligible without pastors like Kyle who not only read what we write but think they find what we write important for the life of Austin Heights Baptist Church. Theology, after all, is a church discipline, and if it does not reflect as well as shape the actual practices of congregations like Austin Heights then it cannot help but be just more opinion or, even worse, another academic subject.

    That you wanted me to preach on this anniversary of Kyle's ministry with you (admittedly, after you could not get Will Campbell) means a great deal to me. Yet, it is always a bit awkward to preach before folk you do not know, and the awkwardness tempts you to speak in generalities that might apply to any situation, but as a result make no difference to anyone. Ironically, I suspect that you know me better than I know you because you have had to endure Kyle quoting me in his sermons and in the *Shepherd's Staff*. In fact, I fear that some of you may have heard enough to develop a healthy dislike of me on the basis of what you have learned from Kyle. Moreover, I fear that what I am going to say today may do little to mollify the negative impressions you may have developed.

Of course, I do know you a bit. I am, after all, a Texan, so I know what it means for East Texans to have a pastor from West Texas. Paula and I are also avid readers of *The Shepherd's Staff*—an interesting name for a church newsletter, and that has everything to do with what I have to say to you today. The shepherd's staff is the sign of the office of the bishop. Bishop is not exactly the favorite office of Baptists (even though there is a Baptist church in Durham called Cathedral Baptist Church). Has Kyle been secretly planning to become the first Baptist Bishop? I can only hope that to be the case.

Some of you may suspect that Kyle has such ambitions because of his sermon style. I have read many of his sermons as well as papers he has written. Kyle is not one to hide his views. Now, I know you do not always agree with Kyle. Indeed, I expect some of you find him far too outspoken, if not blunt. East Texans, after all, are more Southern than Western. I often note that one of the most calculated forms of cruelty ever devised is Southern civility. Southerners control you by never telling you what they think or want. Kyle, Westerner that he is, tells you what he thinks (and he thinks a lot!) and what he wants. I give you great credit for putting up with him because I know Kyle is not always easy to take. But then, the Gospel is not easy to take either.

Of course, it is usually assumed to be a mistake to identify the Gospel with a minister. Having to live with Kyle is one thing, but living with the Gospel is something altogether different. I know, for example, that some of you no doubt put up with Kyle because you love Jane and the girls. When Kyle gets going on why Christians have to be non-violent, or on why he has trouble with both the fundamentalists and the moderates, or on why the people at Austin Heights are too satisfied with themselves because you are not fundamentalist and you are political liberals at least when it comes to race, you put up with all that because, on the whole, he is a pretty good guy, and he has Jane and the girls. Yet, you would be a bit shocked if Kyle actually suggested that how you respond to him indicates your relation to Jesus Christ.

I suspect that Kyle has not explicitly said to you that your relation to him is constitutive of your relation to Christ; but I hope that he believes that to be the case and may even from time to time say it. It is hard to make such a claim about the status of the ministry because in general to be a minister in our society is to be in a devalued profession. That is why we expect above all else for ministers to be nice. If you do not have to work for a living, we lay folk assume that at least you have the time to be nice. That is why being in the ministry in our time is a little like being nibbled to death by ducks. People called to the ministry want to do the right thing. But, since no one knows what they are supposed to be doing, those in the ministry too often end up as glorified social workers, trying to respond to the infinite needs of the congregations they serve because it is clear they have nothing else to do. That is, to be a minister today is to be a tingling mass of availability that too often turns to self-hate because those in the ministry cannot believe they are letting the people they serve so misuse them.

Of course, I know this may be more true of ministers in the more liberal mainline Protestant traditions than for Southern Baptists. I was once sitting next to the wife of a Southern Baptist minister at the annual dinner of the Council for the Retarded in South Bend, Indiana. I asked her how they liked South Bend, and she said, "Not very well." I noted that the weather is indeed terrible, but she said it was not the weather. She told me the problem was that people in the North just did not know what it means to be a Southern Baptist pastor or the spouse of a Southern Baptist pastor. They were from Charlotte, where, as you know, to be a Southern Baptist pastor is to be king. Indeed, I have always said it is unclear who started to look like whom first—whether Southern Baptist pastors in Texas started looking like Texas politicians or Texas politicians started looking like Southern Baptist pastors. But, they turn out to be the same kind of people. In fact, they often also secretly own the used car agency and the funeral home in town.

Now, I know Kyle well enough to know that in his ministry he has avoided being either a glorified social worker or a Texas politician. He has been about building Austin Heights into the body of Christ. Jane and the girls are no doubt important, but you have put up with him for ten years because you know that everything Kyle does he does because God matters. Moreover, the God that matters for Kyle's ministry is the God we Christians worship: that is, the Father, the Son, and the Holy Spirit. Kyle has no use for that vague and sentimental god that most of us keep around to insure that our lives are meaningful. The God that is witnessed to in Kyle's sermons and ministry is the God who is found nowhere else than on the cross of Christ. Only that God is a God capable of saving the world from the powers that would destroy our lives. That, moreover, is why you have brought me here to celebrate your ten years with Kyle, for it is not Kyle we celebrate but rather the God that makes those ten years make sense.

That is why I suggested that how you respond to Kyle is but an indication of your relation to God. By "you," I do not mean you as isolated individuals, but rather as the body of Christ constituted by word and sacrament. To the extent that you are that body, you must expect Kyle to represent Christ in your lives. An extraordinary claim, but one I believe required by our scripture for the morning. Listen again to Paul:

> You know for yourselves, brothers, that our visit to you was not fruitless. Far from it; after all the injury and outrage which to your knowledge we had suffered at Philippi, we declared the gospel of God to you frankly and fearlessly, by the help of our God. A hard struggle it was. Indeed, the appeal we make never springs from error or base motive; there is no attempt to deceive; but God has approved us as fit to be entrusted with the Gospel, and on those terms we speak. We do not curry favor with men; we seek only the favor of God, who is continually testing our hearts. Our words have never been flattering words, as you have cause to know; nor, as God is our witness, have they ever been a cloak for greed. We have never sought honor from men, from you or from anyone else, although as Christ's own envoys we might have made our weight felt; but we were as gentle with you as a nurse caring fondly for her children. With such yearning love we chose to impart to you not only the gospel of God but our very selves, so dear had you become to us.

Unbelievable! Paul, it seems, identifies himself, his very person, with the Gospel. "God has approved us as fit to be entrusted with the Gospel," so that we have imparted "to you not only the gospel of God but our very selves." These are not exactly expressions of humility. What would you think if Kyle said that of himself? "God has entrusted me with the Gospel

Callings: The Ministry and Other Offices

so that my very self makes God present to you. Indeed, if I fail in the ministry then your salvation is in doubt." I suspect that you would think if Kyle expressed such views, he would have gone around the bend. But, I am telling you, not only is that exactly what Kyle should think about his ministry, but also it's what you should hold him to. For, if the Kyles do not exist and churches like Austin Heights Baptist do not exist to make Kyle's ministry possible, then we are indeed lost.

You may well say, "But Paul is Paul and Kyle is Kyle. Paul was an Apostle. Kyle is just another self-generated Southern Baptist pastor who, having nothing better to do with his life, went into the ministry." I am sorry but such a view just will not cut it. If Kyle does not stand before us in the lineage of Paul, then his ministry is unintelligible. When Kyle was ordained, he was made more than he otherwise could be because he was made part of the apostolic office. That office matters. Otherwise, why would Paul have argued so strongly that he also was an apostle? Paul and Kyle make Christ present to us, thereby making it possible for Austin Heights to make Christ present to Nacogdoches, Texas.

Now, I am aware that this may be getting far too serious on a day when we want to be happy. But then, what is supposed to make us happy is that in spite of everything God has called us into his church. That we are so called, that we believe that we have been made part of God's salvation through Austin Heights Baptist and Kyle's ministry, means that we also have to recognize that we are a bit odd. We are not like everyone else in Nacogdoches. We are Christians who believe that everyone in Nacogdoches needs to come to Austin Heights Baptist to see what God's salvation looks like: outside Austin Heights Baptist church there is no salvation in Nacogdoches.

That sounds arrogant, even intolerant, but in a world that has made God into a generalized thing in service to human desires, the proclamation of the Gospel cannot help but sound arrogant and intolerant. Of course, we still live in a world in which people think it is a good thing to be Christian as long as you do not believe that others ought to believe what you believe. But, that world, that world of tolerance, is beginning to come apart. Christians will be forced to discover, whether we like it or not, that we are different. The difference is as simple as discovering that our minister is much more important than who is president of the United States. Our salvation does not depend on who is president, but it certainly depends on the ministry of the church. I suspect that most of us, like Moses, even the youngest, will not live to travel to this new landscape of Christian existence. But, God has graciously let us see with our own eyes this new day, thus making it possible for us to die happy in the knowledge that God continues to care for the world through the ministry of his church.

You may well be thinking, "Hold on, you haven't preached on the text from Matthew. We like the love commandment. After all, what makes us Christians is that we are people of love. Even Paul says that it was with 'yearning love' that he imparted the gospel to the Thessalonians." But that love, the love by which we love our neighbors and ourselves, is the love gained from God's love of us. Love is not some generalized emotion; it rather names our specific relation to God, a relation that is first and foremost determined by God, not by us. Such a love, moreover, is the love made possible by the one who is David's son and alone can be called Lord. God has raised a prophet in Israel for Moses to worship. The new prophet not only has seen God face to face but also is God's face. His name is Jesus. We worship Jesus because he is the second person of the Trinity, who emptying himself became one of us even to dying on the cross. Ask yourself: if Christianity is but the message that we ought to love one another, then how did Jesus end on the cross? He ended on the cross because the world does not want to acknowledge that any love—even the love of a nurse caring fondly for her children—is accursed if it is not forged by the love of God.

Of course, you rightly love Kyle because Kyle's ministry among you has been fruitful. You, moreover, rightly expect Kyle to love you. But, you also expect him to tell you the truth, which is but another way to say that you require him faithfully to preach, baptize, and preside at the Lord's table. So, it is a right and good thing that we celebrate Kyle's ten years at Austin Heights, but it is a good and better thing that Kyle's ministry requires us to praise the God that has called Kyle, like Paul, to be entrusted with the Gospel and who, thus, does not speak to us in flattering words. So, thank God Kyle exists and thank God Austin Heights Baptist church exists making Kyle's existence not only possible but necessary so that we might rightly worship the God of Jesus Christ.

Sacrificing Priests
A Sermon on the Occasion of Rob MacSwain's Ordination
February 2, 2002
St. Mary's Church, Kinston, North Carolina

Malachi 3: 1-4
Psalm 84: 1-6
Hebrews 2: 14-18
Luke 2: 22-40

You do not have to be crazy to go into the ministry in our day, but it certainly helps to be a bit off center. What a terrible job. The only task I think may be worse is to be a principal in any public school. Both positions put anyone who occupies them too close to their constituency. To be a priest or a principal means you necessarily have the most politically demanding job in our society because you cannot escape having to listen and interact with those you are pledged to serve. That is why most politicians in American life want to be in the Senate. We do not elect real people to the Senate. We elect commercials. As a result, senators become fictional agents serving an equally fictional electorate.

The ministry, therefore, becomes one of the last institutions shaped by the habits of direct democracy. Persons in the ministry have to respond to the needs and desires of real people. They must do so, moreover, under the disabling presumption that they do not work for a living. After all, we lay folk assume that they only work two or three hours on Sunday. Admittedly, there are those committee meetings, but such meetings are not more than one or two nights a week. Moreover, everyone is always in a hurry to get home to see Carolina lose again. As a result, most people in most congregations do not have the slightest idea what ministers do with all the extra time they have on their hands. What a cushy job.

Of course, it does not feel like a cushy job for those who are in the ministry. Because they and their congregations are not sure what they are supposed to do, they end up doing a little of this and a little of that, and before long they just feel little. After a few years, many in the ministry feel like they have been nibbled to death by ducks. It is not clear why their ordination vows commit them to being "good with the youth," but someone has to be good with the youth, and since they do not work for a living, it might as well be them. Unable to say "no," the minister becomes a prisoner to the infinite needs of a people who are products of a society that has trained them to believe that life has no limits. The minister often becomes the only one left to take care of us when we discover that we cannot do everything we wanted to do. That is why it becomes so important for anyone in the ministry to be a "caring person"—a role not easy to sustain for a lifetime.

The loss of any clear sense of what the ministry is or should be about reflects the confused state of the churches. To be ordained today is to be ordained in a church in ruins. That the churches, for example, are being torn apart over questions surrounding homosexuality suggests that we have a problem much deeper than that issue in and of itself. I often joke that the Methodists may split over the issue of homosexuality. Methodists can split because we have always confused church unity with bureaucracy. The Episcopal Church lacks sufficient organization to split. The Episcopal Church will just crumble, which is but an indication that whether we like it or not—and I do not like it—we have all become Congregationalists.

One of the reasons the debate surrounding homosexuality is a sign of a troubled church is not that we are debating homosexuality, but that the debate is not the kind of debate Christians should have. Too often, the terms of the debate mimic the way the debate is carried on in secular contexts. Thus, we are told that it is wrong to deny anyone his or her rights, as if rights language is first order Christian speech. We simply seem no longer to be able to have a theological argument. I suspect the reason we cannot carry on the debate theologically is that we have lost confidence that theological language can do any real work.

Our loss of confidence in theology may be correlative to the loss of the church's social status and power in American society. Relegated to the "private," the church is not expected to represent an alternative to the American way of life. The church, of course, is expected to stand for peace and justice, but if Christians get too specific about what peace or justice might actually entail, they are reminded that when it comes to politics the church should not take sides. That is why ministers train themselves not to have strong convictions about anything. Rather, people in the ministry should be "thoughtful," which means they can see so many sides of every issue tht they are permanently immobilized.

I am quite well aware that this may seem an extremely odd way to begin an ordination sermon. Am I trying to talk Rob out of being ordained? Of course, I am not trying to talk him out of being ordained. After all, nothing I have said is news to Rob MacSwain. Indeed, I suspect that he could well add some worries of his own about the state of the contemporary church and its ministry. He has, after all, seen the worst—English Anglicanism. Anyone who has moved from Lambeth Palace to Kinston, North Carolina, in the same year surely knows everything he or she needs to know about that form of Christianity called Episcopal.

My little catalogue of ecclesial worries is not meant for Rob, but for us who witness his ordination. What a remarkable and wonderful thing will be done here. Rob MacSwain will be made a priest of the church of Jesus Christ. A church that, for all of its faults, God refuses to abandon, making possible our setting aside some to be sacrificed so that we may be made part of God's sacrifice for the world. Our ability to go on as the people of God has been made possible by God's gift of himself, God's promise that when Rob celebrates Eucharist there is nothing we can do to stop God from showing up.

In Malachi, we are told that God is sending us a messenger to cleanse the temple, to purify the priesthood, to make the offering pleasing to God. This is a dangerous text to read at an ordination. Such a text might tempt us to think, given the compromised position of the church, that we should expect Rob to be a messenger who burns like a refiner's fire and cleans like fuller's soap. A heroic role for the newly ordained, but the church does not need heroes. We need priests. The church needs priests because we no longer wait for such a messenger. He has come, and his name is Jesus Christ.

Moreover, as we are told in Hebrews, he did not come to help angels but rather to help people like us. Rob's priesthood is possible not because of any of his admirable qualities, but because through cross and resurrection Jesus is now our great high priest. In Jesus the sacrificed and sacrificer are one, freeing us from the slavery brought by our fear of death. All other sacrifices—sacrifices to family, to country, to noble ideals—are but idolatry if they are not disciplined by this one great sacrifice. Whatever else Rob may be asked to do for the church, all that he does must gain its intelligibility from the sacrifice of the altar.

What could be more significant in a world at war, in a world of such great injustice, in a world dominated by the fear of death, than for the church of Jesus Christ to designate one to do nothing else than attend to the acts that make the church the church? Do we not believe that the world's salvation is bound up with our participation in Christ's sacrifice? Some say that the world was changed on September 11, 2001. That is not true. The world was changed during Passover in 33 A.D. That is why there is no more significant response to September 11, 2001 than a people who resolutely gather to participate in God's sacrifice for the world.

Too often, I fear that some think our sacrifice to be an attempt to appease a God who is mad as hell about our unfaithfulness. We lift up the body and blood in the hope that we will not be punished. As a result, we forget that it is God, through his Son, who has been sacrificed on our behalf. The good news is that God has not chosen to save us without us. Through the Holy Spirit, we are made one with Christ in Eucharist so that the world may know that all sacrifices have been brought to an end in this one great sacrifice.

Thus, we can confidently ask Rob to sacrifice his life for our good because we know nothing is more important than the sacrifice he will enact, time and time again, on behalf of the world. What an extraordinary act of hope this ordination gestures. Rob is a bright and good young man. God knows there are a thousand avenues he could pursue that would give him a rewarding career. God, however, has claimed him through our asking him to sacrifice his ambitions, his life, so that the church might be a witness in and to the world, that no thing we do is more significant than the celebration of the sacrifice of the altar. In that sacrifice all our foolishness, all our confusions about the church and her ministry, are subjected to the refining fire of Christ's cross. Whatever reform the church and her ministry need can only come from what God does to us through word and sacrament.

I think that it is not accidental that those who recognized the child Jesus to be the one "destined for the falling and the rising of many in Israel" were old. They were not only old, but they were also as patient as they were filled with hope. They were confident that God would send his messenger to redeem Israel. As witnesses of the vows Rob takes to be a priest, may we be at least as patient and hopeful as Simeon and Anna, for in spite of our unfaithfulness, in spite of how unattractive the ministry may seem today, God has not given up on us or the world. It turns out God did not just send a messenger, but in Jesus Christ, through the Holy Spirit, we have been made participants in the message. We are the "good news." We thank God for sending us Rob, but even more we praise God for sending us the Son who alone makes intelligible what we do here today.

On Milk and Jesus
A Sermon for the Installation of Dr. Gerald Gerbrandt
as President of Canadian Mennonite University
September 28, 2003

Deuteronomy 6: 20-25
Romans 12: 1-3

Once upon a time, I found myself at Iowa State University where I was to deliver a lecture. My habit at the time was to get up before dawn to jog the campus. During my run I passed a large and impressive building that looked like a Greek temple because of the large columns that fronted it. As was also my habit I promptly got lost and ran longer than I had intended. The sun was up when I came back by the building that had so impressed me. I stopped to get a better look at the building, only to discover that above the columns chiseled in the granite was the word *MILK*. This was a building devoted entirely to the study of milk. I suppose there is no reason to wonder why this might be the case. Iowa does milk.

I thought, moreover, what a wonderful way to organize the knowledges of the university. Imagine how interesting it would be, for example, if the Department of English were a division of the School of Milk. If that were the case, I suspect (at least at Iowa State), a good deal less about postmodernism would have been heard. Even better, what a wonderful thing it would be for the Department of Philosophy to be under the Dean of Milk. Think about the learned papers that might be written trying to determine if milk is a primary property. You may think that I raise these possibilities only as a joke, but I am deadly serious. I see no reason that universities should be organized by the schools and disciplines as we now know them. I think a curriculum centered around milk makes a lot of sense.

What does this have to do, however, with this great day on which Dr. Gerbrandt is installed as President of the Canadian Mennonite University? I hope it might mean that in the future when a jogger is running around this campus he or she might see above a building (a building that we know will not look like the Milk building at Iowa State because such a building would not be an appropriate expression of Mennonite modesty) the name *JESUS*. Mennonites do Jesus. I hope, moreover, that name might be just as important for the formation of knowledges at CMU as the word milk might be at Iowa State.

I can make such a suggestion, of course, because I know you are Mennonites. In the letter inviting me to speak at this installation service, I was asked to "speak for approximately twenty-five minutes in which you inspire us with a vision for a Christian university that is rooted in the church; or as Dr. Gerbrandt recently put it, 'a university of the church for the world.'" A happy assignment, but one that is made easier because you are Mennonites. You are "Jesus People." I realize that Mennonite modesty also requires you to confess that you are not always "Jesus People," but at the very least you can make no sense of your history, as told by the *Martyrs' Mirror*, if you are not Jesus people.

I must be careful, however, not to idealize Mennonites (as I am sometimes accused of doing). I quite understand that it is a mistake to think that Mennonites are clear, at least among themselves, about what it means to be Mennonite. You know you are not Catholics. You may or may not be Protestants. You are sure there are deep differences between German Mennonites and Russian Mennonites, though the differences keep shifting. I am also aware that at least some Mennonites think there is little difference between milk and Jesus. John Howard Yoder never tired of holding Mennonite feet to the fire by suggesting that, in spite of the Mennonite disdain for Constantinianism, you have managed to create your own form of Constantinianism. It is called "farm culture." I suppose John was right to think that milk could be as worldly as the military. Let me be clear, however: these remarks do not imply that I am taking the side of city Mennonites against farm Mennonites. As a mainstream Protestant, I know better than to try to help decide arguments between Jews arguing with Jews and Mennonites arguing with Mennonites.

Of course, Mennonites know they are pacifists. Or, at least you remember that when your children ask you what the statutes of the Lord mean, or why so many of your forebears died rather than take up the sword, you must explain that your ancestors believed that Jesus would not have them kill, even if they and those whom they loved had to die. Moreover, the Mennonite conviction that you cannot take up the sword depends for its intelligibility on the name Jesus. After characterizing and assessing twenty-seven forms of pacifism in *Nevertheless*, John Howard Yoder described the "Pacifism of the Messianic Community," the position he thought should be that of the Mennonite church by observing, "This is the only position for which the person of Jesus is indispensable. It is the only one of these positions which would lose its substance if Jesus were not Christ and would lose its foundation if Jesus were not Lord" (134). So, it is Jesus, not pacifism, that must appear on any Canadian Mennonite University building equivalent to the Milk building at Iowa State.

Jesus, moreover, is the basis for any determination of the world to which we are not to be conformed, for the world is not just there to be seen. We must learn through discipleship to Jesus what is world and what is not. We would like to think that the world is relatively easy to spot. Being pacifists tempts us to assume that "world" names any behavior implicated in violence. That may not be a bad place to start, but we must remember that our commitment to nonviolence does not insure that our lives are free from being implicated in violence all the more pervasive because it is invisible.

We are here today to celebrate the work of the university. Next to the church, I love no institution more than the university. Universities have sustained my life. I am grateful for the good work I have been given to do by the university. I should like to think, moreover, that the university is a civilizing institution that makes peace more likely. The university is the institution of memory that not only answers our children's questions but also teaches them the right questions to ask. The university is that institution that creates the space and the time for people to read *The Iliad*, study Plato and Aristotle, discover that rocks have a history through the discipline of geology, marvel at the different beauty of insects through the study of biology, and learn to appreciate the complexity of the physics of milk. What a privilege it is to be able to spend one's life in the university.

I believe, moreover, that the church has a stake in universities. In *The Spirit of Early Christian Thought*, Robert Wilken observes that by the fifth century, "Christianity was beginning to create its own distinctive culture. As Christian intellectual life matured, Christians sought to give expression to their faith in art and architecture, law and politics, and the writing of history and poetry" (213). Moreover, Wilken reminds us that the poetry Christians produced was not esoteric explorations of personal angst, but poetry such as the Te Deum that could be sung by the congregation:

You, the glorious
    choir of the apostles,
You, the admirable
    company of the prophets,
You, the white-robed
    army of martyrs
do praise.

Christians produce a material culture. We do so because we worship Jesus. We insist that our God has been revealed at a particular time, in a specific place, and in a very real human being. As a result, Christians have thought it possible to create images of our Savior. Wilken notes that because of the Christian refusal to "spiritualize" Jesus, Greeks and Romans—that is, people who had the presumption that they represented what all people should want to be—found Christians parochial. Christians failed to live up to the aspirations of a universal and cosmopolitan culture because they were so tied to this Jewish savior. Christians were clearly backward people.

Of course, in time, Christian parochialism replaced Rome. Christians, it turned out, had a more effective force to take over the world than Roman legions. They were called monks. Those monks, moreover, produced much of what we now identify as great literature, philosophy, theology, music, science, and art. They also produced the university. So, it seems that Christians have had a stake in universities, but, of course, Mennonites are not just another form of Christianity. You are among the most parochial of Christians. Jesus is the name that appears on your lintels. No matter how hard a Mennonite may work to help students learn to love Dante, the Mennonite does so knowing that Dante is important only to the degree that Dante helps us learn the significance of the name Jesus.

This means that, as you begin this great adventure called the Canadian Mennonite University, you have your work cut out for you. You will be tempted to be just another university with a Mennonite difference, but if Jesus is carved on the lintels of your hearts, it is not sufficient for you to be "just another university with a Mennonite difference." Your difference will necessarily go all the way down. The great treasure called the Christian tradition, the beauty that Christians in the past have created in praise of our Creator, the philosophical and theological reflection necessary to keep the Church focused on our Lord, cannot be taught here without reminding your students that often the Christians who produced such beauty produced people who killed your ancestors.

Mennonites are the Jews of Christianity. So, it should not be surprising that you share much with that great Jewish Marxist, Walter Benjamin, who observed:

> Whoever has emerged victorious participates to this day in the triumphal procession in which the present rulers step over those who are lying prostrate. According to traditional practice, the spoils are carried along in the procession. They are called cultural treasures, and a historical materialist views them with cautious detachment. For without exception the cultural treasures he surveys have an origin which he cannot contemplate without horror. They owe their existence not only to the efforts of the great minds and talents who have created them, but also to the anonymous toil of their contemporaries. There is no document of civilization which is not at the same time a document of barbarism.

Benjamin's sobering judgment tempts us to think that concentrating on milk might be better than teaching students to read Plato, but, there are also violent and nonviolent ways to milk cows. At the Canadian

Mennonite University it will even be necessary to chisel Jesus above the building dedicated to milk. Paul urges us to present our bodies as a living sacrifice, holy and acceptable to God. Nothing is quite as bodily as milk. The infant that suckles the mother's breast is but a reminder that the renewing of our minds does not mean our bodies can be left behind. At the very least, this means that if you are to build up that body which is Christ's through the work of the Canadian Mennonite University, you cannot invite a strong distinction between the theoretical and practical work of the university.

You have a lot going against you as you begin the work of forming this university. You are Canadian and you are Mennonite. You cannot get much more parochial than that, which hopefully will save you from the assumption that there is something out there called a university setting standards that you need to imitate. Do not believe that for a moment. Your task is to be what you must be if you are to be faithful to your history as Canadians and Mennonites. If you do that, you may well teach those of us who teach at universities that think they have to be like every other university how interesting it can be when Jesus makes a difference for how you understand the production of milk—or how you teach history, study physics, or practice art.

That last sentence is where I should probably stop, but to do so would mean that I failed to raise the fundamental challenge presented by Paul's admonition that we are not to be conformed to this world. If Benjamin is right that every document of civilization is also a document of barbarism, then why should we—and, in particular, Mennonites—bother to have a university at all? Does the very existence of the Canadian Mennonite University suggest that you have already become "conformed to this world?" I am well aware that this is not an unknown question in the Mennonite tradition. The very existence of your Amish brothers and sisters is the living embodiment of that question. Neither they nor the question they represent can or should be suppressed. I do not believe, moreover, that you think the question can be or should be suppressed.

Indeed, I believe that Christians who work in the university must begin each day by asking God in prayer if we should do this day what we did yesterday in service to the university. Yet, my prayer is different from your prayer because my university is not in Canada and is clearly not

Mennonite. Indeed, the relation of Duke to that pale form of Christianity called Methodism with which Duke was originally associated is at best understood at Duke to be "part of our history." So, Duke University serves the Rome of our day, the United States of America, and we therefore assume that someday the Canadian Mennonite University will want to be Duke.

Dear God, I pray that you may be saved from that fate. You have a great deal going for you. You are, as universities go, poor. That means you will need the support of people that milk nonviolently so that you might teach nonviolently. Neither the administration nor the faculty of the university will determine the future and the faithfulness of the Canadian Mennonite University. They will make a difference, but the difference they make will only be possible if a church exists that wants that difference made. Only if a people exist who have not been conformed to this world—because they have been for the world God's living sacrifice—only then will it be possible for the work that you must do here to be truthful. What a wonderful and frightening task you have been given, Dr. Gerbrandt. You, and the wonderful faculty of the Canadian Mennonite University, will be in my prayers. You will need all the prayers you can get.

Callings: The Ministry and Other Offices

Rev. Emmanuel Katongole, a Roman Catholic priest from Uganda, teaches in the Divinity School at Duke. He raised money to have a well dug in his village. He wrote the following letter, to which I responded with the following prayer:

Dear all,

I write with great excitement and joy in my heart to announce that the gift of water has finally flowed in Malube, my village. It was yesterday at 5:15 pm when the final pipes were inserted in the over 90-meter borehole, and the final fittings were secured. I was there to pump the very first pitcher of clear flowing water. Looking on were a number of village folks, including a number of children, whose joyful amazement could not be concealed. Within minutes, many of the children had run home and returned with jerrycans and other containers to draw water. Before long, there was . . . a long line of yellow plastic jerrycans, waiting to collect the water. A number of children also wanted to try their hand at borehole, but the chairman of the well committee, afraid that the kids might easily turn the borehole handle into a swing, selected only four or five kids for the honor! He also called a village meeting, slated for this afternoon, for the village to vote on the modalities and regulations of use, which the committee has been working on. It was nightfall when I left to return to the university last evening, but many of the village folks were still at the well site, some drawing water, others simply watching or talking about the incredible gift of water—clear flowing water.

Disrupting Time

As I made the slightly-over-50-km-journey from home back to the university last evening, I could not but think of the joy and 'future' that has been brought to the people, especially the children of Malube by the tremendous gift of water from Christians and friends so far away, but who from now on will ever remain close to the hearts and lives of the people of Malube. Many thanks to you all for your generosity, but more especially for your friendship to me, which has made this gift possible.

My love and prayers, as always,
Emmanuel.

Give us happy hearts, Lord Jester. May we delight in your creations, your beautiful compelling world, created to make us need one another. May we see, may we feel, may we be overwhelmed with the wonder of water—a common enough, a simple enough aspect of your creation. But, the common is not easily seen, particularly by people like us. We are complex people, whose complexity is required if we are to negotiate that complexity we call "now." But then, you send us Emmanuel who reminds us of the wonder of water. We confess that we find Emmanuel a mystery. Why is he so happy? He is a priest, a Roman Catholic priest. Priests are not supposed to be happy, but he is happy and he is happy because he is a priest. He wants us to be as happy as the children of Malube. That is to ask much. We are, after all, complex people. So, we ask you, Lord of Delight, to help us rejoice in your incredible gift of water—clear, flowing water—water that made us your baptized. Transfix our lives with the lives of children that we may be for others what Emmanuel and his village are for us—Christians.

Joy, sheer, uncomplicated, unmitigated joy is what I think I long for. To be made happy—sure, that is what I want. Augustine famously began, "Our hearts are restless until they find rest in you." But, in the same moment that I desire to rest, to be at peace, I fear that You, Creator God, might actually give me what I desire. Rest sounds too much like death. I fear that the peace-rest beckons because if I do not keep moving how will I know that I am not dead? Do this, do that; constant "doings" which make me always "too busy," but at least by "doings" I am protected from your peace. Yet, the more I move, the busier I become, and more deadly I become—numb to my own feeling. Advent, learning to wait with your people, the Jews, comes interrupting my busy life. Dear God, for your Son's sake stop me long enough so I might learn to wait, and so taught, may I even learn to delight in the time that is the music of your creation.

Disrupting Time

A Prayer before the Duke Youth Academy:

Good God, Lord, what you have done with your people, the Jews, and with us, your church, makes clear that you did not create us to be at home in this world. I confess, however, that I like my routines. They give me comfort; I not only know where I am but what I am doing. So, I must have been out of my mind when I agreed to give this lecture, a lecture on death, in particular your Son's death, to your people who do not know they were born dying. Do not get me wrong, Father of life and death: I do not blame them for living as if death-free life is possible. After all, it has only been recently that I have understood death is not a theoretical possibility even for me. So, what we have here is a classic setting for the manipulation our lives call a "communication problem." Of course, you have always faced that problem with ear-deaf sinners like us. We even find a way to ignore the Word you shouted in the cross of Christ. Clever creatures you made us, capable of denying your Spirit's visible words of body and blood. They are just symbols, we say. Well, if any communication is going to happen here, we will need the weirdness and wildness of your Spirit to make these words as frightening and true as the redemption of all that is in the cross and resurrection of Jesus. May that death frighten us to death, and so frightened, may we live.

Callings: The Ministry and Other Offices

Dying, Dale Aukerman, rejoiced he had lived.

Dying, Dale Aukerman, rejoiced he had lived "to see crocuses blooming again." Growing even closer to death, dear Jesus, you sent him a baby swift falling down the chimney of the stove. He said, "I caught it with a dish towel, gazed at it closely, and took it to the porch. When I opened my hand, it soared high above the walnut trees, even though it had never flown before." Why is it, Lord of crocuses and swifts, that we so often can see your glory in each rock and tree, in each bird and plant, when we are dying? Why does our living tempt us to think, "If you have seen one sparrow, you've seen them all"? Do I fail to see the crocuses because I know that to see them, to really see them, requires an unselfing that feels like death? Give us clean eyes to see how all that is glorifies you. So seeing, may we discover that in our deaths is life—a life so fearfully beautiful that we are no longer tempted to lead fearful lives.

Disrupting Time

The Dying of Jim McClendon

Denying death, death overwhelms us, leading us to live deadly lives. Yet, you are the resurrected Lord who would pull us, kicking and screaming to be sure, into life. A living life that makes possible, that makes necessary, the contemplation of our death, and even more, the death of those we love. Jim McClendon is dying. The fierce integrity of his life and work, his stubborn desire to say no more or less than the truth, has made us better by helping us name the lies that feed on our fear of death. Jim always worked slowly, painstakingly worrying over every sentence as if it would be the last he would write. He could take the time for the task of theology, knowing that it matters little whether his theology was finished or not because given theology's subject, the task is never finished. He is, after all, a baptized Baptist, so he knows he is not finished until he is received into the company of your saints. So, may Jim die happy and so may we happily remember him.

Jim McClendon died on October 29, 2000

Bodily Lord, Jim McClendon worked hard, carefully, and tirelessly to remind us that you are a fleshly lover. He feared you and, therefore, fearlessly saw and helped us see you in those who suffer in the lives of Clarence Jordan and Martin Luther King, in the anarchy of Dorothy Day, in the music of Charles Ives and Charlie Parker, in the fierce seriousness of the philosophy of Wittgenstein, and in our own lusts and loves. I always suspected that you gave Jim a Catholic body but forced him to live a baptist life—a small "b" Baptist life. He loved good wine; he loved sailing; he even loved, God help us, California. But, all his loves became in his life a witness to your desire to have us live at peace, to enjoy one another and you. You have now transformed him, made his body anastatically a member of your communion of saints, perfectly at home in your love. We will miss him, but we rejoice that you have given us his witness, this wonderful life, to help us see the beauty of your peace.

Disrupting Time

Only you, Wily Lord, must know whence he came. His life must have been a surprise even to himself—a privileged kid, one educated, lacking the "common touch," yet destined to be one of your decisive witnesses. We celebrate his life, but we fear that such celebration may distance him from challenging our own lives. Sainthood, even among Protestants, can work to free us from any assumption that we also may be called to be holy. Dietrich Bonhoeffer was an unlikely disciple, but you somehow found a way to help him rediscover that we are all called to be disciples of Jesus. We, therefore, give you thanks for his life, his witness. May we, like him, learn that quiet courage necessary to be people of truth. Help us be plain-spoken and honest witnesses so that the world may know what a wonderful thing it is to be loved by You and to love you.

Callings: The Ministry and Other Offices

On the Death of Dana Dillon's Father

Death, stark sudden death, hovers over our lives unrecognized. Then, there it is, felling those we love. John Dillon died this morning. We know him through the goodness and grace of his daughter, Dana. Through her, we are pulled into the sadness of his death. We never know what to say, so save us from saying silly things. Rather, give us the grace to be with Dana. May we not overwhelm her with our sympathy. Let us speak the truth to one another. Death is frightening, and every death but reminds us of our own death—a death that may be around the corner. May our fear of death not be blind to the good lives names like John Dillon name. Without such lives, we are lost. So, we give you thanks for John Dillon who lived so well that Dana rightly mourns. May we mourn with her.

Disrupting Time

On the Death of Eileen Quirk

Words, I pray for words.
Words that will comfort but not lie.
You are, after all, the Logos.
"In the beginning was the Word."
But then your Word, your Jesus, died a comfortless death.
So dying, we are schooled by His life
to see the terror that stalks in the everyday.
Yet, through His death and resurrection
we believe you have given us the gifts
that make the everyday possible.
Gifts as everyday as a woman's love of a man,
a love that erupts,
making place for a stranger child.
The beauty of such gifts,
the wonder of such gifts named Eileen,
resists any words that in the face of her death would comfort,
that would too quickly restore normalcy.
In the absence of comfort
make it possible for us to give thanks for her life,
her loves, her joy. Teach us how to go on
befriended by those she loved,
sadness shaped by the courage that was her life.

On the Suicide of an Eleven Year Old Son

Darkness spreads, how does life go on? The suicide of a child, eleven years old. No explanation explains. No words can or should comfort. Cross darkened Lord, all I know to do is pray that You will be present to Jim and his family. Make me present to them through prayer. Help them not be temped to the comfort offered by half-truths. God, life is tough, life is hard, but you are a tough God. Somehow, help us stumble through the terror, the darkness, knowing that you will find us in the dark.

Two Remembrances

John Howard Yoder
December 29, 1927-December 30, 1997

A Remembrance

The 1978 *Festival Quarterly* had a feature called "Winter Profile" that featured John—he had an uncanny knack for getting into the important magazines. The interviewer asked John if he enjoyed his significance. "Oh, time has passed me by," he responded. (We are told he said this "without feeling.") "I won't strategize making sure I get my monument. I got caught between the H. S. Bender generation and the Willard Swartley generation."

Obviously failing to get Yoder to be introspective, the interviewer tried again by asking Yoder whether he was happy. "I haven't found it very useful to ask that question." We are then informed that Yoder is quite critical of the cult of happiness, seeing it a form of cultural conformity. But yes, he is thankful and does not feel hurt or oppressed. He notes, "So far our children haven't hurt their parents much. I have tenure. And I don't think I'll run out of Anabaptist sources." Yoder, we are told, said this with a tone of peace and just a pinch of resignation, noting "I'm not concerned with building an empire."

Quintessential John Yoder—which, of course, puts us who have come to praise him in a tough spot. As Christians, we already know better than to try to insure that we will not be forgotten—not that, as the Stoics knew, that is a fruitless task—but because it is the deepest sign of unfaithfulness. Any attempt to insure our memory in this world is the denial of that community that John now enjoys, that is, the communion

Disrupting Time

of saints. Yet, we also know that John would not like for any of us to say anything about him that seemed to make him more important than what he most cared about, that is, God's nonviolent kingdom. Michael Cartwright observed that John has certainly gone to extreme lengths to make sure he did not have to respond to the *Festschrift* some of us are in the process of preparing.

Yet, like it or not John changed my life, and I, at least, think he ought to be held accountable. Reading Yoder made me a pacifist. It did so because John taught me that nonviolence was not just another "moral issue," but constitutes the heart of our worship of a crucified messiah. Of course, I know that John was never quite sure what to make of having so convinced me. At an event arranged by Jim Burtchaell, John and I were giving short accounts of our life and work for new graduate students at Notre Dame. As usual, John described himself as a dilettante having no real field but having written for many years in defense of Christian nonviolence. He confessed that as far as he knew, he had only convinced one other person, meaning me, and I could tell he felt a good deal of ambiguity about that "accomplishment."

In truth, I know that I was a burden for John. In speech and writing, John was exacting. He had the kind of exactness only an analytic philosopher could love. He never said more or less than needed to be said. "I haven't found it very useful to ask that question." Notice he did not say it is wrong to ask whether one is happy; he said it is not useful. Such exactness can be quite exasperating. I, on the other hand, love exaggeration. Why say carefully what can be said offensively? John, committed as he was to the ministry of careful speech, I know found exasperating how I said what I thought I had learned from him. Yet, he was patient with me, which is but an indication that he knew he even had to treat me nonviolently. I know that at times it was not easy.

I suspect that was particularly true given my polemical style. Among Mennonites, John was certainly not "laid back," but how he approached those "outside" as well as critics of his work was quite different. I kept getting into fights because of what I had learned from him, and he would then suggest it was my fault. In truth, I think he was right about that. He knew how to be nonviolent because he had all those witnesses, those Anabaptist sources, to teach him how. So, rather than showing the incoherence of this or that version of just war theory, John would find a way to hold advocates of just war to their own best insights. He really lived and thought believing that God is to be found seeking those whom we think to be our deepest enemies. As one new to the practice of non-violence, I know that is a skill I can at best only dimly imagine, much less desire to live as John lived it.

This means that we simply cannot with truth accept his claims to his own insignificance. For many of us, Mennonite and non-Mennonite, he changed our world through how he lived and what he wrote. In particular, I have been asked by Lisa Cahill, President of the Society of Christian Ethics, to say that our coming meeting will not be the same with John missing. We will continue to expect to see that enigmatic figure on the back row taking notes but saying nothing, though it may be a session on a topic that he knows more about than anyone in the world. (And it goes without saying that most sessions of the SCE were about matters he knew more about than those writing the papers.)

So, in an uncharacteristicly Yoderian mode, I think it best to end with some of John's words. This beautiful and exacting passage, beautiful because of its exactness, comes close to the end of *The Politics of Jesus*. I believe that what John said in it is not only the heart of his work, the heart of Christian theology, but also the heart of what it means to live as a disciple of Christ:

> The key to the obedience of God's people is not their effectiveness but their patience. The triumph of the right is assured not by the might that comes to the aid of the right, which is of course the justification of the use of violence and the other kinds of power in every human conflict; the triumph of the right, although it is assured, is sure because of the power of the resurrection and not because of any calculation of causes and effects, nor because of the inherently greater strength of the good guys. The relationship between the obedience of God's people and the triumph of God's cause is not a relationship of cause and effect but one of cross and resurrection.

Therefore, it must be true, as John puts it, that "the people who bear crosses are working with the grain of the universe." A life capable of such writing is not replaceable, but the very God that makes such a life possible we can be sure will send us new, and no doubt quite different, John Yoders. At this time, however, let us rejoice that God gave us this life, this bit, of the grain of the universe.

Tommy Langford

I have to tell people that I am committed to Christian nonviolence. I have to tell people that I am so committed because my life belies that conviction. You do not have to be around me long to know that I am not exactly a peaceable guy. As far as I know, Tommy never said he was a pacifist. He did not have to say he was formed by the habits of Christian non-violence because he was so obviously a person of peace. He was so, I believe, because he really was, as we Methodists put it, sanctified, which is but a reminder that sanctification names the rest, the habits, shaped by the conviction that God has redeemed the world through the cross and resurrection of Jesus Christ.

Tommy did not have to change the world. He knew that the world had been changed, so that in a world as dark as war and petty as the envy between academics, he could take the time to listen, for surely the virtue of peaceableness begins with the ability to listen—to receive. Tommy could listen. He could hear what the other person was saying, not what he might want them to say. He could listen even to me. I would rage into his office, an office I now happily inhabit in the hope that his memory will inhabit me, and he would absorb my rage. He never told me to calm down. Rather, I calmed down because he listened.

Yet, there was nothing sentimental about Tommy. In fact, there was a hardness at the center of his soul. Because he knew his life from minute to minute was sheer gift, he also knew that neither he nor those he loved could afford to live lies. So, he sought to be truthful, knowing that truth but names the arduous discipline that we must undergo if our speech, and the life our speech makes possible, is to be a truthful witness to the

God who is the beginning and end of our existence. After all, what good would a peace be that was not truthful.

Joy, the exhilaration that is ours in response to God's grace, was the hallmark of Tommy's life and theology. He loved theology, he loved the church and the university that made his work as a theologian not only possible but necessary, because he knew that the God he worshiped as a Christian delights in truth. That is why, I think, he never feared asking himself or us questions to which neither he nor we knew the answer. He was quite capable of making himself and his friends uncomfortable by truthful questioning. He was so because he knew that whatever answers we might have in life must reflect our willingness to befriend and be befriended by the mystery that the other exists not to please ourselves, but because his or her existence pleases God. How else can we explain Tommy's extraordinary ability to be a friend with people as peculiar as you and me without ever wanting us, in the interest of getting along, to be anything other than who we are.

Tommy's life was, in truth, a witness to the God that he knew could be trusted to be the truth. So, I know no more fitting way to remember Tommy than to ask you to join me in a prayer of thanksgiving for his life:

> Lord of life and Lord of death, we give you thanks for the life of Tommy Langford. Tommy was wise, but he was so because you taught him early how to wait, to be patient. He lived knowing each day could be his last, so why not use that day to plant a daffodil, talk with a friend, read a book, or pray—all of which for Tommy may have been the same thing. Of course, he did much good work. He ran the Divinity School and even the University, whatever it may mean to run those things. More importantly, You somehow gave him the gift not only to put up with fools but to love them into being at least less foolish. God we will miss him. He was one of those who makes the world better because he is just there. He could just be "there" because he never doubted that whatever he was he was nothing without You. So, help us left behind. May we learn to be there for one another. One last thing—when his eyes are closed he often really is listening hard to what you have to say. He listened to us, thereby, making it possible for us to shout, to celebrate, this life with a grateful amen.

Hauerwas on Hauerwas: Interviews

Zion's Herald Interview with Stanley Hauerwas
Stephen Swecker

ZH—Let's take off on a title from one of your pieces that I just ran across, "How Did Karl Barth Learn To Be Karl Barth?" How did Stanley Hauerwas learn to be Stanley Hauerwas?

SH—Largely by accident. I sometimes say that when I go out to give a talk, and I'm picked up at the airport, I suddenly realize the people who are picking me up aren't picking me up. They're picking up something called "Stanley Hauerwas," someone with which I have trouble identifying because I still think of myself as a little half-assed Texas kid trying to make good. I didn't come from an educated family. I was the first member of my family to go to college. So, I always have the idea that somehow I'm pulling the wool over people's eyes intellectually because if you're a theologian today, you never know enough. And so I find it absolutely puzzling that I'm Stanley Hauerwas. I know I've written a lot of books and that I seem to have a fairly large reputation. But, quite frankly, none of that comes home to me.

ZH—Who were you before you were Stanley Hauerwas?

SH—I was raised a bricklayer. I labored up until I was 15 or 16, and then I learned to lay brick. Hard work has always been who I am. I don't think I ever took a class in which I was the smartest person in the class. There was always someone smarter than I was. But, I work hard, and, if I have a gift, it's a kind of intellectual homing device to go into the central issues, and I don't avoid them. I try to have something to say.

Disrupting Time

ZH—In the early 1970's my advisor at Boston University, Paul Deats, once told me that I needed to read some Hauerwas. He described you as a "sophisticated thinker." You couldn't have been much out of graduate school yourself then.

SH—That's true. Paul was a terrific guy. He was an old Protestant liberal, but he was also a pacifist. So, he had convictions that would drive him into positions that you might not otherwise be driven into.

ZH—What were you doing back then that would have made that kind of impression on Paul Deats?

SH—I don't know. I guess I'd given papers at the Society of Christian Ethics. I was an inadequately trained academic in the sense that I didn't understand early on that you were supposed to have "fields," and that if you had a "field," you didn't need to read in another "field." So, when I went to college it was like this wonderful cafeteria that had all these wonderful things that I could read, and so I did. I didn't make a strong distinction between philosophy and theology, political theory and novels. I just read anything that pleased me and that I thought I needed to take account of. I didn't read them because other people read them. So, I became much more sophisticated than I knew I was in terms of my varied education.

ZH—Time recently named you America's "best theologian." Based on your writing on so many moral and ethical issues, I had always thought of you primarily as an ethicist, not a theologian.

SH—Well, when I was in divinity school I didn't think of myself as a Christian. I just was trying to find out if the stuff was true. I took a course from Julian Hartt who was a great philosophical theologian at Yale. It was systematic theology. He made the point in numerous ways that people tend to think of Christian convictions as a kind of primitive metaphysics that you map over world views of how things work. In contrast, he thought of Christianity fundamentally as practical discourse. So, I decided to become an ethicist because I thought that was the way to do theology. I never thought of myself as a Christian ethicist, however, although that was where I was primarily writing and publishing. I've always thought of myself as a theologian, because what I've wanted to do is show how theological language works to tell us the way things are and how it shapes us to be the people we need to be to know the way things are. I want to remind us that learning how to become a creature is every bit as complex as learning what justice is. It's a way of reminding us that theological claims are practical down to the very bone.

ZH—Why is that important?

SH—As a matter of fact, it turns out to be very important. The way disciplinary divisions work within the modern university and seminary is intellectually corrupting. For example, theologians think that students learn to read Scripture in Old Testament and New Testament courses, and therefore we theologians don't need to use Scripture as part and parcel of the way we do our work. I try to defy that in every way I can. And, I refuse to accept the assumption that you need to know all the historical, critical scholarship behind the text to know what the text means.

ZH—Say more about that in terms of the work of people such as John Crossan or Marcus Borg.

SH—Yeah, I have very little use for the Jesus Seminar. The Jesus Seminar's idea that somehow or other through the use of historical methodologies they're going to get to the "real Jesus" is absolutely crazy. The real Jesus is the resurrected Jesus, and the idea that somehow, since these Gospels were produced later and therefore are not newspaper accounts, and therefore they're not getting the real Jesus, is just absolutely conceptually crazy. It's crazy! So, I think that the Crossan- and Borg-like presumptions that they are quasi-scientists reconstructing the real Jesus that we can somehow believe in is a sign of the intellectual corruption in modernity that assumes that historians know what they're talking about.

I don't think historians know what they're talking about at all.

ZH—What are you passionate about today? What are the things that really stir you?

SH—Right now, I'm really concerned about whether the Braves should resign Maddox or not. I want to resign Maddox, I think, and so I can be real passionate about baseball. Baseball's a game of failure, and so there's always the next game, next year, and you're always having to worry about that. I really care about that. I'm passionate about my marriage.

I have a wonderful marriage. It sustains me, and I love my wife deeply. I oftentimes say that one of the cruelest things that we're required to do as Christians is to love one another, even in a marriage. I don't assume that love is necessarily intrinsic to marriage, but I am one of the most in-love people in the world, and it's a terrific thing. I care deeply about that.

It is something of a surprise for me, but probably one of my deepest passions is teaching. I didn't start off to be a teacher. I didn't think about it. I knew I had to do it to make a living, but I taught in order to have an excuse to think and be a theologian. Over the years, I've learned, particularly with my graduate students, that they invigorate my life, and I have a deep passion for the friendships that are formed through teaching.

ZH—Where do you find your deepest experience of community these days?

SH—In friendships. I think that's dangerous, too, for Christians. I think that our deepest identification should be in our church. Simply because we're in our church doesn't mean that we need to be friends with everyone in the church in order for that to be our primary locus. My sense of the matter is that for many of us today our churches and our commitment to the church find expression through the necessity of friendship beyond the church. My friendships are all over the globe, and I work to keep up contact. I dictate my letters. I don't do e-mail because e-mail just doesn't give me the kind of interactions I want, and so it takes me almost an hour a day to answer letters. It's well worth the time as far as I'm concerned.

ZH—Karl Barth is said to have summarized his many volumes of work by saying, "Jesus loves me, this I know, for the Bible tells me so." Is there any such summary of Stanley Hauerwas?

SH—As a matter of fact, I just finished the Gifford Lectures. The book's out, by the way, titled *With the Grain of the Universe* (Brazos Press). I argue in the Gifford Lectures that Karl Barth is the great natural theologian of modernity. I spent a lot of time trying to trace down that quote you mentioned. He seems to have said it at Union Theological Seminary in Richmond when he was in America. And I know that the Americans kept wanting Barth to say something profound. It was driving him crazy, so he said something like, "Jesus loves me." What Barth was doing was resisting any notion that the Gospel could be summarized, and I would always resist that notion, too. I think reductive accounts of the Gospel are destroying Christianity. For example, if you asked that question to many Christians they'd say, "Well, the heart of it is that God is love." Well, I just think that's a lie. I mean, I hate that. You'd think Jesus, after coming back from the temptations, which we know weren't really with the devil but with the existential nothingness of life, that after coming back from the desert he says, "You know, I've really had an insight. I think I really got it. God wants us to love one another." Now, why would anyone kill anybody if that's what this is about? "God wants us to love one another." Obviously, that doesn't cut it, and so I think the attempt to find a heart or an essence of what you're about is something that must be resisted.

ZH—You've said that the center of the Christian life is nonviolence. Do you still believe that?

SH—I do think it is central, but I didn't want to become a pacifist. I hated becoming a pacifist. I still don't like it. But, I was reading John Howard Yoder, and Yoder absolutely stunned me with his argument that nonviolence cannot be separated from Christology. It is at the very heart of how you understand God's care of the world through the person and work of Christ. And so, it wasn't like I believe in Jesus and then I can make up my mind about being nonviolent or not, but rather, nonviolence is the way that God has redeemed the world through cross and resurrection.

ZH—How have the events of Sept. 11 influenced the way you think about nonviolence?

SH—I think, of course, it's just horrendous what happened, and there's nothing that excuses or justifies it. After the first stunned couple of weeks, though, I find the rise of "God and country" just frightening. I think it's not because people are bad that we get this patriotic fervor. It's because people are lonely and desperate. They feel violated, and they hope to overcome the violation through identification with the cause of democracy. That's very dangerous. I think Americans sense the fragility of this social order, and because of the fragility of it they can become very repressive. Unfortunately, Christians have become so identified with the "we" of America that we don't know how to think as Christians, and so what I try to do is help us think as Christians. What would it mean for Christians to say to George Bush, "You're facing a tough set of decisions. On 'just war' grounds you need to be engaged in a police action at most to arrest bin Laden, and B-52's are pretty crude policemen. If you have to pursue international means that take time and may even fail, you will not find yourself abandoned by Christian response. We're there to support you in that." The problem, of course, is that most Christians in this society are so American that they don't have the patience for this response.

ZH—How in the world, then, are we going to continue to carve out space for dissent?

SH—Right now, dissent has just evaporated. There is no dissent. When you just try to bring critical questions to bear, people get extremely frustrated with you. I don't think enumerating all the bad things America has done in the world is the way to go. It doesn't excuse or justify what happened, but it does mean that this is surely a time for stock taking. America is Rome. We're an unchecked power. We do not yet know what it means for America to be America without an enemy.

ZH—You write in your 1983 book, *The Peaceable Kingdom*, that "none of us know the depth of our violence." Is that a word that we need to hear again at this time?

SH—Oh, I certainly do think so. Classically, as Augustine showed, evil is nothing. Evil is always parasitical on the good. That's the reason why we don't know the depth of our evil, because we don't know the depth of our good and how to discover the violence that lies in our loves. I wrote a sermon years ago called "Hating Our Mothers As The Way To Peace" based on Luke 14:26. I pointed out that few people kill out of sheer malice. The people that are bombing in Afghanistan now are killing in the name of their loves, of protecting their parents, their wives and their husbands. Violence lies in our loves. And how to love without being implicated in violence, it seems to me, is an ongoing challenge that is never over. We think, "I'm loving, and there just couldn't be violence in that." But there is violence surrounding it, imbedded in it. I oftentimes say people never lie to each other more readily than in marriage. And why is that? It's because the intimacy that we've achieved is so precious and fragile we're afraid of saying anything that might make us lose it. But in trying to protect it, we lose it. That's why Christians, even in marriage, can tell one another the truth because we're married. We know we're committed to lifelong faithfulness, and therefore the marriage is more determinative than the personal interactions at any one moment. What great good news.

ZH—In the *The Peaceable Kingdom* you write, "The peace of God, rather than making the world more safe, only increases the dangers we have to negotiate."

SH—Another way to think about that is, as I say, the courageous know fears the coward will never know. Because, if the courageous don't know fear, they're just foolhardy. They must know fear and yet act in the face of their fear. Insofar as they act courageously, they will confront the world with challenges the world does not want to have challenged. And so, the very fact you're courageous means you make the world more dangerous. The same is true of people committed to nonviolence. You can make the world more violent because the world does not want its violence exposed. Yet, you must confront your violent brother and sister because you do not want them to be inured in their violence.

ZH—If I hear what you're saying, then a nonviolent person should always be in a state of confession and contrition.

SH—Yes—and also conflict. You want to occasion conflict that otherwise would simply have been pushed under the rug.

ZH—How about it? Do you enjoy conflict?

SH—I don't know. People say I'm a very polemical guy, which I assume I am, and that I seem to represent a position that many people love to hate and oftentimes love to hate me for it. I don't know that I enjoy that. I do love argument, and I'm good at it. I guess I love it because I'm good at it. The truth of the matter is, and this sounds self-congratulatory, but I'm a lover. I mean, I love people and I love the life I've been given. I'm not about division as the first way of life for me, although I can't deny that I've created one hell of a lot of conflict. Indeed, I'm not apologetic at all about it. I like the arguments I've occasioned.

ZH—You're a little bit ahead of the curve in *The Peaceable Kingdom*, and by the curve I mean what people are talking a lot about today as spirituality and the spiritual disciplines. You were talking about that in 1983, and wanting to relate a Christian ethic to the spiritual life. What do you have to say about that today?

SH—I gave up on the language of spirituality because the dunderheads got it. Spirituality became a way to talk about a universal need that we all have that can be expressed through any religion some way or the other. This kind of individualistic, getting-myself-right with the powers of the world, I'm not sympathetic toward it. I am very sympathetic toward exercises that have been well explored through centuries of Christian practice that are now embodied in wise people that can teach you how to go on. But, never forget, the Devil's a spirit and the Devil can appear as a spirit of discernment, and so you have to be very careful with that. I wouldn't want to be among the proponents of spirituality today. I'm more than willing, though, to talk about prayer, fasting, obedience, silence. I regard spirituality as learning how to talk. What that means is not being afraid of your "first order" religious convictions, and that you can just say it. The Psalms are "first order" religious convictions, so I take a lot of comfort from the Psalms.

ZH—You also speak in *The Peaceable Kingdom* about the Christian ethic or the Christian way of life as learning not only how to talk but also how to see and how to envision the world. How do we do that?

SH—You can only act in a world you can see, and you can only see by learning to say. It is an ongoing discipline of maintaining accuracy in speech so we are not misled by the falsehoods that lie in our language. How to preserve truthfulness of speech is an ongoing activity. You've got to learn to become articulate, and you need to be part of rich linguistic cultures to do that. I do think learning to see and being able to describe accurately the world in which I live is an ongoing task that is never finished.

ZH—Last question, and I would expect nothing less than the truth from you on this. Is Stanley Hauerwas the best theologian in America?

SH—No, not even by a long shot. The American theologian that I read that has taught me more than I'd otherwise know is Robert Jenson, who's a Lutheran theologian at The Center for Theological Inquiry in Princeton. And I think there are some young ones who are just wonderful. He's not an American, but I think Rowan Williams, the archbishop of Cantebury, is clearly one of the great theologians around. Bruce Marshall, who's just gone to SMU, is a man of stunning abilities. And so on. I say it's a horrible time for the church but it's a pretty good time for theologians. We don't have anything to lose. God has robbed us of status. It's terrific. We don't have anything left but to try to say the truth, so we don't have to try to underwrite social pretension or status. The church is free, thank God.

Faith Fires Back:
A Conversation with Stanley Hauerwas
Duke Magazine Interview with William T. Cavanaugh

William T. Cavanaugh: You're an academic, but you're more than just an academic. You have a keen pastoral sense, and you do a lot of things beyond the academic world—now in the media, but before that just talking to little churches here and there. And your writing style is really less academic as well. Can you say a little about that?

SH: If I were any of my colleagues at Duke, I would be very tired of "Hauerwas." In fact, I am very tired of "me." I have no idea how I have suddenly become famous, but I am not happy about it. Indeed, when a theologian, particularly in the kind of world we live in, becomes famous, you have an indication that a mistake has been made. Our subject after all is God.

Of course, to be a writer is an invitation to narcissism. How to escape narcissism is very difficult. The very effort to escape only increases our self-fascination. My only hope is having friends who remind me what I am supposed to be about. Indeed, friendship is very important not only for my life but in how I think about ethics. In the *Nicomachean Ethics*, Aristotle says that for the upbringing of children as well as for living well, we need a society of good laws that teach us to desire the right goods rightly. But when such practices are absent, we must depend on friends. That seems to me to describe our situation very well.

Which is why one of the tasks I have undertaken is to change how we think about the moral life. I have tried to redirect attention to the importance of the virtues as well as the narratives that make the virtues intelligible for understanding "ethics." Of course, such an emphasis I thought necessary to recover how Christians should think about their lives.

It is so difficult in America for Christians to imagine what it might mean for them to be Christian. We have lost the first-order speech necessary to shape our lives. I have tried to help Christians recover our speech habits by writing little books for laity. I wrote a little book with [Dean of the Chapel] Will Willimon—who said he was going to make me famous—called *Resident Aliens*, which created a readership I would not normally have as an academic. It turns out Christians were surprised to be told they are odd.

Will and I have tried to follow that book with short books on the Lord's Prayer and the Ten Commandments. These books try to de-familiarize those extraordinary texts in the hopes Christians can appreciate the radical character of our faith. I have even written a little book called *Prayers Plainly Spoken* to try to show that, when we pray, about the worst thing we can do is try to be pious. I hate prayers that begin, "Oh, God, we just ask you..." About the worst thing Christians can do is try to protect God when we pray. Read the Psalms. You do not have to protect God. That is why God is God and we are not.

WC: You're also famous pedagogically. One of the famous pedagogical tricks that I like is not explaining things, letting the audience figure it out.

SH: I do not know if not explaining is a "trick," but I do try to say some things in a way that invites resistance and further reflection. I think I learned the importance of that way of working from Wittgenstein. Wittgenstein teaches you that the unsaid must remain unsaid. You only discover what must be left unsaid by thinking hard about what you have learned to say. I also try to develop epigrams that have been forced on me by positions I have taken whose implications I slowly come to understand.

For example, I say, "The first task of the church is not to make the world just. The first task of the church is to make the world the world."

I know that sounds offensive to most people, Christian and non-Christian. Of course, I want it to be offensive. I am trying to challenge the assumption that Christianity is acceptable in modernity as long as it supports moral and political causes most people assume anyone should support—e.g., democracy. Such a view assumes that God can be entertained as a possibility as long as we keep it to ourselves. So I try to remind Christians by such an epigram that—as Augustine maintained—the church's first political task is to worship the true God truly.

WC: It occurs to me, the way you're talking, that your attention to aesthetics is underappreciated. You really have a very keen aesthetic sense. You're constantly thinking about the attraction of it, and that it's got to be an attractive message that lures people into it by its beauty, in a sense. And oftentimes its beauty comes in its brokenness.

SH: Beauty is the heart of goodness and the moral life. I learned that originally from Plato and later from Iris Murdoch. I do not write about "aesthetics," but rather I try to remind us of the beauty we no longer notice because we have lost the wonder of the everyday. I have recently written a piece for the Catholic Liturgical Society, "Suffering Beauty," in which I suggest that just to the extent beauty calls us beyond ourselves we "suffer."

The Catholics had asked me to speak about liturgy as moral formation, but I thought that very way of putting the matter was a mistake. Liturgy is not something done to provide moral motivation. The liturgy is how the church worships God and how from such worship we become a people capable of being an alternative to the world. That is why the language of the liturgy is so important. Nothing betrays the love of God more than the inelegance of the language Christians use in their worship. Some Christians seem to think we can attract people back to Christianity if we try to compete with TV, but when you do that you have already lost. The only result is that Christian worship becomes as banal and ugly as the rest of our lives.

I think it would be terrific if on entering a church people would think, "This is very frightening." God, after all, is frightening. Recently, I had a debate about the interpretation of the Bible at Southeastern Seminary in Wake Forest. One of my graduate students, a Roman

Catholic, went with me. When we entered the church where the debate was to be held, she said, "Wow, is this someone's living room?" So "fundamentalists" want to make people feel at home—a home, moreover, that looks more like the living rooms of the 1950s. It is no wonder you are tempted to put an American flag in such "sanctuaries," because at least the flag adds some color. Unfortunately, the colors, at least when they are part of the same piece of cloth, are not liturgically appropriate.

WC: One of the things that makes it hard for a lot of Christians to swallow your message is that you say the church doesn't have a social ethic, it is a social ethic. How do you deal with the division between what is and what ought to be?

SH: God's given us all the time we need to patiently help our congregations be what they can be. That's the way you want people formed, because that's the way the Spirit operates. If you help people discover the violence in their lives, though, don't expect to be honored. One of my favorite epigrams is that Christians are not nonviolent because we believe our nonviolence is a strategy to rid the world of war, even though, of course, we want to make the world less violent. But rather, Christians are nonviolent in a world of war because we cannot imagine anything else as faithful followers of Christ.

WC: If you were a pastor of a church right now, what would you be saying after September 11?

SH: People say that September 11 forever changed the world. That is false. The year 33 A.D. forever changed the world. September 11 is just one other terrible event in the world's continuing rejection of the peace God made present through the Resurrection. And therefore, how Christians narrate this event will be different than how other people narrate this event.

Christian willingness to kill other Christians in the name of national loyalty is surely one of the assumptions many Christians assume is not to be questioned. Yet no assumption has contributed more to the accommodation of Christianity to secular ways of life than the presumption that Christians have no problem with war. For Christians to be nonviolent is not just another political position, but rather at the very heart of what it means to be Christian, of what it means to be human. I believe God created all that is with the desire to be nonviolent. We are not meant to be killers. That is why we have to be trained to kill. God wants us to be in love with God and with one another in a manner that our differences challenge our self-imposed desires. Christians in America have difficulty responding to September 11 as Christians because we are more American than we are Christian.

The current identification of God and country is very troubling. Let me be as clear as I can be—the God of "God and country" is not the God of Jesus Christ. Yet this is not a development that began with September 11. One of the issues before American Christianity is whether the God we worship is the God of Jesus Christ.

American Christians simply lack the disciplines necessary to discover how being Christian might make them different. For example, after the Gulf War, people rightly wanted to welcome the troops home, so they put yellow ribbons everywhere including the churches. Yet if the Gulf War was a "just war," that kind of celebration was inappropriate. In the past when Christians killed in a just war, it was understood they should be in mourning. They had sacrificed their unwillingness to kill. Black, not yellow, was the appropriate color. Indeed, in the past when Christian soldiers returned from a just war, they were expected to do penance for three years before being restored to the Eucharist. That we now find that to be unimaginable is but an indication how hard it is for us to imagine what it might mean for us to be Christian.

The current outpouring of patriotism, I think, is an indication of how lonely we are today. We are desperate to be part of some common endeavor. I am often called a communitarian, but I think that is a mistaken description. I am not for a rediscovery of community as an end in itself. Such a rediscovery can be as dangerous as it can be good. Rather, I try to help myself and others rediscover what it might mean if the church constituted our primary loyalty.

WC: A lot of us have heard you say these sorts of things before. We were sort of surprised when you appeared in The New York Times and you said that we ought to think of this as a police action. Two questions: First of all, when you say "we," are you now making policy recommendations? The second question is how do you, as a pacifist, think about "police action" as opposed to "military action"?

SH: If I said "we" in The New York Times, it just means I wasn't thinking, and I was on a linguistic holiday.

WC: Now, I'm not going to let you off the hook that quickly, though, because clearly the church does not undertake police actions in that sense.

SH: Right. When I used the "we," I identified with those who would assume the perspective of the nation-state. I am a pacifist, but I gladly try to help those who say they want to fight a "just war." But the "just war" tradition is as demanding as pacifism. For example, it is by no means clear on just-war grounds that you can fight a just war against terrorism. Let me be clear. The people that attacked the World Trade Center clearly wanted to terrorize Americans. They wanted quite clearly to frighten us, quite literally, to death. But it is not clear to me, if you are a just warrior, that it is helpful to call how you respond a "war on terrorism." What they did was murder. If it is murder, on just-war grounds, you do not want to kill the perpetrator. You want to arrest the murderers.

The question then becomes, what kinds of forms of international cooperation do you need to develop or be able to arrest whomever you think has been responsible for this? You may not be the arresting agent yourself. I raise this consideration to help those committed to just war be imaginative in terms of their own commitments.

"War" is not just "there" if you are serious about just war. Just war is an attempt to create the institutional form prior to a war occurring so that, if it occurs, it will be more likely that war will be just. Now, if a war is not just, what is it? In several interviews about September 11, I said, "Well, you know, if the World Trade Center was terrorism, so was Hiroshima and Nagasaki." There were no great military targets there, and even worse than Hiroshima and Nagasaki was the firebomb raid on Tokyo. It was awful; we killed more people in the firebombing of Tokyo than in Hiroshima and Nagasaki combined. And when I made that point, reporters said, "Well, that was war." To which I responded, "Well, you know, you can murder in war."

I want to know on what grounds you use the honorific description "war" if a war is not just. We think you can distinguish war from murder—what are the presuppositions that allow you to think that you can do that? And there's a very important issue of whether just war is basically a series of exceptions from a general stance of nonviolence, or whether it assumes that it's always about justice in a world of war.

That latter presumption assumes war is never an attempt to establish a world free of war, because if you want justice in the world as we know it, you've got to be ready to kill somebody. I respect that position, but then I want to know, what do you mean by the word "justice"? How can you have justice? What kind of justice are you talking about in international conflicts? Those things need to be explored, and they're not being explored. What I think oftentimes happens is that we get a military and a State Department whose policies are shaped by geopolitical consideration of realist foreign policy, and then they want to fight a just war. It's too late. It's too late, because you've already let yourself be led into the world in a way in which you say the first responsibility of the president of the United States is to protect the United States' self-interest. And what I want to know is how the United States' self-interest is determined by justice.

QUESTIONS FROM THE AUDIENCE: What's the point of defending a society that's built on spending? We've been terrorized by Madison Avenue for how long, through the television and such?

SH: Be careful with that kind of language. You've been manipulated by Madison Avenue—I'm not sure you've been terrorized. And it's very important to get the description right. As a response to September 11, for academics to roll out all the things that they've thought have been wrong with America and American foreign policy is—the word I'm close to is "duplicitous." It is morally inappropriate. Nothing that America has done in the world justifies, excuses, or explains September 11.

It is therefore all the more important for us—and this is the use of the word "us"—to try to understand why it is that many people in the world find it satisfying that this has happened to America. On September 11, America was dragged kicking and screaming into the world. We think of ourselves as global, but our globalization has remained safe within the boundaries of our ocean, and now the reality of the world has been brought home. We're mad as hell because we didn't really want to deal with this kind of world on an everyday basis. It's a very important moment for national self-examination, and I would like to be as helpful to that as I can as a Christian. If you are a pacifist, you don't want to withdraw—you want to be as helpful to your neighbor as you can.

AUDIENCE MEMBER: Talking about the unity of the church, how might that apply to the current debates concerning homosexuality in the United Methodist Church, in the Presbyterian USA church, and the Reconciling Congregations movement within the United Methodist Church?

SH: The problem with debates about homosexuality is they have been devoid of any linguistic discipline that might give you some indication what is at stake. Methodism, for example, is more concerned with being inclusive than being the church. We do not have the slightest idea what we mean by being inclusive other than some vague idea that inclusivity has something to do with being accepting and loving. Inclusivity is, of course, a necessary strategy for survival in what is religiously a buyers' market. Even worse, the inclusive church is captured by romantic notions of marriage. Combine inclusivity and romanticism and you have no reason to deny marriage between gay people.

When couples come to ministers to talk about their marriage ceremonies, ministers think it's interesting to ask if they love one another. What a stupid question! How would they know? A Christian marriage isn't about whether you're in love. Christian marriage is giving you the practice of fidelity over a lifetime in which you can look back upon the marriage and call it love. It is a hard discipline over many years.

The difficulty, therefore, is that Christians, when they approach this issue, no longer know what marriage is. For centuries, Christians married people who didn't know one another until the marriage ceremony, and we knew they were going to have sex that night. They didn't know one another. Where does all this love stuff come from? They could have sex because they were married.

Now, when marriage becomes a mutually enhancing arrangement until something goes wrong, then it makes no sense at all to oppose homosexual marriages. If marriage is a calling that makes promises of lifelong monogamous fidelity in which children are welcomed, then we've got a problem. But we can't even get to a discussion there, because Christians no longer practice Christian marriage.

What has made it particularly hard is that the divorce culture has made it impossible for us to talk about these matters—and many of you know, I'm divorced and remarried. It has made it impossible for us to talk about these matters with an honesty and candor that is required if you are not to indulge in self-deceptive, sentimental lies.

For gay Christians who I know and love, I wish we as Christians could come up with some way to help them, like we need to help one another, to avoid the sexual wilderness in which we live. That's a worthy task. I probably sound like a conservative on these matters, not because I've got some deep animosity toward gay people, but because I don't know how to go forward given the current marriage practices of our culture.

[DEAN JONES ASKS:] Bill has asked you a lot of questions, others have asked you several questions. What question would you like those of us gathered here to be thinking about as we depart from here?

SH: What do I need, or what do we need, to be a community of friends that can not only tell one another the truth, but want to be told the truth?

A Conversation with Stanley Hauerwas
Image
Interviewed by Brian Volck

BV: I wanted to start off by asking about narrative theology and how you became interested in it.

SH: I don't like the name "narrative theology." One of the things I've resisted is having any qualifier other than "Christian" in front of theology; neither do I like "theology of's." Christian theology is reflection on God and God's claiming us through Jesus Christ; all those qualifiers are the attempt to sell the package on other grounds. I don't want there to be anything called "narrative theology."

I first got to thinking about the significance of narrative in a course on Christology taught at Yale by Hans Frei. This was before he had written *The Eclipse of Biblical Narrative,* so there wasn't much about narrative in the course, but we dealt with the classical, Christological debates. Then we moved into Christological arguments around Protestant liberalism, and the more I thought about it, the more I thought that Protestant liberals—who generally I'm in complete disagreement with—were trying to do something with the old lives of Jesus that classical Christology had lost: to pay attention to the life itself. From a certain perspective it looked like all Jesus had to do was be born, die, and be resurrected, but I got to thinking that there had to be a mistake there. One thing that drives people crazy about the Gospels is that they tell us almost nothing about what Jesus was thinking.

BV: Scripture seems singularly uninterested in psychology.

SH: Absolutely, and there are a lot of bad sermons that try to come up with things for Jesus to think, when really the Gospels are trying to tell us not to think that way about Jesus. The more I thought about it, the more I saw that his life had to be integral to why he had to die. This idea connected with the work I was doing in so-called ethics, trying to recover the significance of whole lives. I was trying to argue against situation-ethics, trying to discover the importance of character and the virtues, and wanted to find a way to talk about continuity that is always about change. Christianity is not about a datum. It's about *change*. The question in Christianity is not how you account for change, but how you account for continuity. Catholicism has always understood that change is inevitable, that even if you think you've finally got your life right, if you try to freeze it, everything around you is still changing. The same is true of Christianity. It requires constant negotiation and renegotiation.

In trying to find a way to think about continuities, I thought of narrative because I've always been a novel-reader. Narrative, with plots and subplots, gave me a way. It can be a helpful means for understanding how we finally receive knowledge of ourselves by God's claiming us through Christ: Christ's life narrates our lives. I always say, you never know who you are until God tells you who you are. Who is more of a de-centered self than a saint of the church? The saints don't know who they are until God tells them, and that's true of us all.

Some time after I started using the category of narrative, it became popular—people were doing a lot of narrative theologies. I was afraid that people were beginning to think that narrative saves, rather than God saves, so I quit using the category as a determinative—a conceptual device—and started speaking more directly. If you press me and ask if I've given narrative up, I'll say no, not at all. It's still a very important set of conceptual moves that can help you think about quite a range of issues that theology should be concerned with. I just don't want to turn it into a new thing. It's not new.

BV: It strikes me that in the Jewish tradition, story and instruction—Haggadah and Halakah—are equally honored, while in the New Testament, alongside the narrative of the Gospels, Acts, and Revelation, there are twenty-one epistles which are largely didactic. The Christian tradition seems reluctant to use story. It resurfaces from time to time, and I'm wondering why that is, and how we can regain our Jewish roots.

SH: Part of my work has been a re-Judaization of Christianity, even though I want to be—and I hope I am—a thoroughly orthodox Christian. I want to believe everything the church believes. One of the temptations for Christians is that because Christianity went to the Gentiles, we want to be able to make our faith intelligible without telling the story of Israel. "Very God, Very Man," as an ontological response to an ontological set of problems from creation onward, doesn't really require you to tell the story of the people of Israel or the continuing story of the Jews. And part of my theological commitment is to show that Christianity is unintelligible without the Jews—in other words, it is particular. The story of Christ is the story of stories, but its universality does not come at the price of its particularity.

Faulkner would sometimes reflect on these matters. A story like "The Bear" is absolutely, particularly *Southern,* determinedly rooted in the land of the South, yet people who don't know dipshit about the South understand it. Literary people sometimes talk about the way that concrete, particular detail gives the reader a sense that "this is my story too"—but you have got to *do work* for it to be your story. Judaism and Christianity are particular in that same way. When narrative theology first came out, some people pointed out that there's a lot in the Scripture that isn't narrative: the Psalms, the Wisdom literature, the pastoral letters. That's true, but everything said in the Psalms, the Wisdom literature, and the pastorals depends on *the* story; in a sense, the Gospels have primacy over the other literatures. The fact that in church we stand to hear the Gospel is a reminder that this is what everything else depends on. And of course the story begins, "In the Beginning was the Word." Where the hell did that come from? Obviously from Jewish wisdom, maybe translated through certain philosophical schools in the ancient world. You might say that the Wisdom literature is not in its first order a narrative, but has now been transformed. The narrative includes all the literatures that are not narratives in their first mode, and so you can find the interrelationship between those different kinds of discourse. And it's not just a question of narrative and everything else; the crossing between genres is an ongoing process.

BV: You were talking about people recognizing their stories in the story somebody else is telling. I'm wondering if that's one of the ways that story instructs which is unavailable to argument.

SH: Those are very hard issues. I've never wanted to undercut the necessity of argument by saying, "Well, let me tell you a story…." I think argument is important, and practices that are integral to significant narrative force you into argument. That's why I find the Rabbinic tradition excellent. I don't like the language of pluralism, but when people are determined to use it, I say, "Listen now, if you want an example of pluralism, it's Rabbis arguing Torah." Rabbis argue Torah because the Torah requires it. Take for example, "Anyone that lies with an animal shall be put to death." The Rabbis say, "Right. Now what does it mean to lie with an animal? How many witnesses does it require?" What God wanted was to create a people who could enter into the discourse—who could argue—and by doing that, discover what a wonderful thing it was that God had chosen them. So I think argument and narrative are in no way incompatible.

Now your question is, can stories do work that arguments can't? I think it's like this: Aristotle's understanding of first principles is oftentimes misunderstood. People think Aristotle believed that with a first principle like the law of contradiction, you first think it up and use it as a test of anything else you might want to say. In contrast, first principles are constituted by discoveries of practices, so you have the axiom and then the practice, but they necessarily come together. Certain kinds of narratives are like that. They're discoveries that you can't make anything else that you're doing intelligible without the narrative. So, in a certain sense people can understand the story where they can't understand the argument. And the story is a *kind* of argument.

BV: You were talking about first principles as a way of justifying particular habits.

SH. That's a crucial part of the argument of my understanding of Christianity. Liberal Christianity is a form of Constantinian

Christianity that wants to give an argument to those who are not Christians that says, "You already believe what we believe. As long as you've got an ultimate concern, that's us!" I regard that as extraordinarily coercive and violent. It is an attempt to make Christianity intelligible without witness, and Christianity can only be made intelligible by one person telling another; it can't be intuited. There's no way you could intuit that God called the nation of Israel to be His promised people. There's no way you could reason yourself to an understanding that God in Christ was reconciling the world. You've got to be told. When people say, "What's all this revelation stuff?" I say, "You've got to drop the idea that revelation is an epistemological category. It's not some kind of special knowledge. Revelation just names what your mother tells you."

Now, one of the problems with witness is that people hear it. Then they tell it back to you, and you think, is that what I said? But the Gospel is not the Gospel until it's been received. That oftentimes works as a judgment on our lives. We haven't really heard the Gospel, but God has the person we witness to hear it better than we have told it or lived it. If that process is at the heart of the Gospel, *then* we're about constant, wonderful rediscovery of what God has done.

BV: I once heard Richard Rohr say that a Christian is someone who has really *met* another Christian.

SH: Oh, that's wonderful. My life isn't all that impressive, but what I know is that Christians have made me Christian, for which I praise God. I don't like language about people "having an experience of God." Do you really want that? I mean, it would scare the shit out of me. I've never had much use for "experience" because our God is known not by "zapping" kinds of modes, but by the creation of space for people to exist in, thereby making life possible that otherwise wouldn't be possible. That's what the church is about: creating that space, being that space. That's grace.

I am not very happy talking about grace either, because it becomes a generalized category. The only grace is Christ. When grace becomes a generalized relationship with God that doesn't require the mediation of Christ and Christ's church, then you're floating right into gnosticism, and I've got no use for that.

BV: One person who frequently creeps up in your writing is the noted Miltonist and literary critic Stanley Fish, which sometimes leads people to accuse you of relativism. What can Christians learn from Stanley Fish?

SH: Stanley's great gift is seeing through the mystifications of liberalism. His article "Liberalism Doesn't Exist" is absolutely brilliant: he shows not that liberalism is true or false, but that it doesn't exist as a position. The liberal epistemological mode, which underwrites liberal political theory, is that one can assume a stance from which one can judge all beliefs prior to having any, which of course is a complete illusion. You don't get to exist prior to beliefs. You're constituted by them. So what Stanley does is provide some wonderful, clear reminders that it's not a question of whether you will or will not have strong beliefs—it's a question of which ones you will have. And then you've got to be ready to argue. Because liberalism, in spite all its claims about wanting to have free exchange of ideas on a level playing field, basically hates conflict. The whole point of liberalism was to kill Christianity, and it's done that by convincing Christians to be liberals. That's what I am trying to convince Christians they should not be, and Stanley provides an arsenal of carefully crafted illustrations showing that presumed neutrality, the assumption that I can secure a place of objectivity, is illusory. The goal of modernity is to produce people who believe they should have no story except the story they chose when they had no story. (I use that language because I'm attempting to give a description of liberalism that liberals will agree to.) They call that freedom. But what they cannot account for is who told them that story.

This is an overly clever way of trapping liberals, but it holds very well with people who have the disadvantage of a university education, because they recognize that modern university education is basically an attempt to talk people out of being redneck Texans and into being fairly tolerant middle-managers for IBM. I want to show them that they traded one story for another.

It's very hard to think well and be wealthy, as we all are in this society, because you never are faced with limits early enough. The wealthy often appear to deserve their wealth because they can afford advantages which hide their limits. They don't come into conflict with people who might question them. Being a wealthy country the way we are is very dangerous to our moral health—that's part of what's going on now. Then people think that by becoming middle-managers at IBM, they've gotten what they chose. It is a horrible thing to get what you want in life. What would happen if you really married the "right" person, or had the "right" children? How would you ever know what life is like, and should be like? At Notre Dame when I taught Marriage and the Family, I taught Hauerwas's Law: you always marry the wrong person.

Of course, you also marry the right person. I think one of the most frightening phrases in English is, "We always had a happy marriage." That just tells me that someone lost early. It suggests that marriage is a consensual relationship that is constantly being renegotiated for the sell-fulfillment of both people, that they can't stand to have conflicts which might threaten the marriage. But the reason Christians can really disagree, even if they're married, is *because* they're married. It's a wonderful freedom where we don't have to live out self-deceptive stories that make the original lust, which was confused with love, what the marriage is about. And I'm for lust! I mean, you know, that's fine.

To really disagree, to be able to have epistemological crises is a great achievement. Most of the time we don't come into disagreement, we just pass like ships in the night. And that's the reason why, when we bump up against one another, all we can think to do is kill each other. People think that pacifists like myself are against conflict, but Christian non-violence is *committed to* conflict: if we can have the conflicts out, then you've got some hedge against violence. Christians have been sent out to the world with the joy of this witness, which means we want to give everyone we come into contact with an epistemological crisis. Of course, this puts us into epistemological crises, too—it makes us rethink who we are. And what a wonderful thing God does for us. It stops life from being just one goddamn thing after another.

BV: You use novels frequently in your writing. I particularly remember Peter DeVries's *The Blood of the Lamb* and Anne Tyler's *Saint Maybe*, and I understand that you've used *Saint Maybe* in classes. I'm wondering how novels inform the Christian life.

SH: I love novels. I didn't come from a cultured background, I remember in college reading *The Great Gatsby* in my freshman English course and just falling in love with Fitzgerald. I hadn't known people like those characters existed. I will use any excuse not to read theology and read a novel. I justify reading novels by using them in my courses—they give students a way to enter an imaginative world in which we see not only ourselves, but Christianity. I think one of our difficulties today is we can't imagine what it means to be Christian. I know I'm not much of a Christian—I live with this stuff everyday and it still doesn't seize my imagination. But one of my deepest loves is Trollope, which usually surprises people. Tolstoy, by the way, thought Trollope was *the* greatest English novelist, even next to Austen and Eliot. Trollope would not have agreed—he thought Austen was the purest, and Eliot the profoundest. But in any case, Trollope shows us a world in which Christianity—conventional Anglicanism, in his case—still worked. To watch conventional Anglicanism work in a Trollope novel is to see it working one hell of a lot better than it does for us.

Also, novels provide a wonderfully inventive kind of help in loving people who are otherwise not very lovable. None of this is to say that the only novels I think are helpful to the Christian imagination have explicitly Christian authorship. I love Updike, who is a Christian, of course—the American literary establishment will never forgive Updike for making the middle-class interesting—but indeed one of my favorite novel forms is detective fiction, which in some ways you can read as decisively anti-Christian, because there's seldom any redemption. I'm a pacifist, and for pacifists the question of whether you want criminals caught and punished is an interesting, important challenge. Murder mysteries can help us to deal with that, I think. Iris Murdoch has been important for me, and I've read every novel she wrote. I read a lot of Joyce Carol Oates. I don't know whether Oates has any religious convictions at all; if she does, they don't show, but her books help me imagine the world I inhabit. It's very difficult to discover the stories that are living through you, or sometimes even to notice them, and I think novelists do help us do this—more than sociologists do, for goodness sake. So a lot of what I'm doing when I read is just trying to get a grip on my life. I love the academic novel. *The War Between the Tates* by Alison Lurie: terrific. I've read all of C.P. Snow. *The Masters* is still one of the great academic novels. I love a good story, so I'm completely promiscuous in my reading. I'm still intimidated by anyone who can write. I think they're smarter than I am.

BV: The last time I looked at Amazon.com, there were fifty-five titles somehow associated with you.

SH: I never think of writing as something I do. People ask me, "How do you do it all?" I have no idea. I read a lot, and the reading and writing do complement one another. I'm almost never without an idea. Indeed, it can be quite oppressive. Some people think that there's no idea I don't publish, but that's not true. Also, since I write so much, I think there's a kind of impression that it's carelessly done, but that's not true either. It may be wrong, but it's not carelessly done. I work very hard at it.

I wasn't born a writer. I've *become* a writer, and it was very hard work. When I started out I couldn't write, and I didn't know you needed to know how. I thought theology was about ideas, and you just wanted to get the ideas out, but being in such a literary culture, I began to understand that writing well matters. It's especially hard to write essays that people both inside and outside a set of discourses will want to read. In my essay collections I try to put pieces with different audiences next to each other—something written for readers who wouldn't know Alasdair MacIntyre next to an essay in which I talk about Alasdair a lot, next to an essay in which he isn't named but whose ideas he embodies—so that a reader could go back and read the first essay again and understand the connections. Serious intellectual work is about showing the connections. I try to do that by writing well and showing that there are connections to be made in one's own life, that indeed it's crucial to make these connections in order to live well. I've worked very hard at becoming a better writer, and I've learned a lot by reading good writers—novelists and essayists both—and watching how they do it. I work very hard on first sentences of essays, just as a novelist works very hard on the first sentence.

I didn't want an academic career; I didn't know it was there to be wanted. When I went through divinity school and Ph.D. work I was trying to make sense for myself of what it meant for me to end up being a Christian. When I went out to teach, I didn't know there were certain journals you should publish in if you wanted a career. I just had these ideas I wanted to get out—and I wanted to convince people. In a certain sense my work has always been about creating a readership, and goddammit, I've done it.

BV: It seems you've proudly borne the title of "tribalist, fideist, sectarian"—which I believe was intended scornfully—and have described yourself as an "in your face" Christian. I'm wondering how you negotiate conversation with those who describe themselves as Christian humanists, who themselves are trying to encounter what they see as the entire cultural tradition.

SH: I think the greatest Christian humanist of our time is Karl Barth. Absolutely nothing human was foreign to Barth. He knew that everything was God's Creation, even if it was in a sinful form. People are oftentimes puzzled by his extraordinary reading habits, his love of Mozart and so on, but I find all that consistent with Barth's Christological center. What bothers me about the notion of Christian humanism is: what created it? If it is a protest against a certain kind of Christian inhumaneness, then certainly it's a good idea. But there is in the idea of Christian humanism a kind of Constantinian strategy that says that what it means to be a Christian is to be a part of a civilization whose continued existence absolutely depends on these literatures. Therefore it becomes crucial to have read Plato in order to know what it means to be a Christian. It's a very serious position that says you need to read Plato—or at least somebody within the Christian civilization needs to read Plato—in order to understand what Christianity is about. I accept that as a descriptive claim. I don't accept it as a normative claim.

How to negotiate Christian humanism in a way that doesn't become a form of cultural imperialism is a serious question today. Christian humanism probably arose around New Criticism and the modernist movement and was located oftentimes around Anglicans who wanted to say, "Oh, yes, I'm a Christian, but I'm a Christian humanist." I worry about that. There are words that certain traditions should not be allowed to use. The Methodists should never be allowed to use the word *experience,* because they had one once, and it was sexual and it was good, and they've never gotten over it. Calvinists should never use the world *covenant* because it can get confused with contract in the modern world. Anglicans should never use the word *incarnation* because they mean God became man and said, "Hmm, this is pretty good." You can't tell the difference between a Unitarian and an Anglican in Boston, because they're both humanists and get along very well without God. Incarnation is not about God saying okay to the human, it is God's transformation of the human into the divine. It's divinization. We're not just about being human. We're about being disciples of God's revelation in Jesus Christ. If that's what you mean by being human, fine, but certain humanisms can lead to a kind of celebration of the way things are that Christians have to be wary of.

Christian humanism is also associated with developments in the modernist movements where you start getting art for art's sake. Art for art's sake oftentimes assumes a kind of romanticism in which art reveals the essential commitments of a culture. This romanticism was clearly strong in Paul Tillich, who has been and remains the great guru of people who are interested in religion and the arts. I don't like those moves generally, because I don't like the mystification of art, where art is turned into something separate from craft. Museums can be very misleading, insofar as they separate art from the actual practices of a people, from serving the enhancement of community. Charles Taylor makes a point in *Sources of the Self* that art became art with the loss of Christianity exactly because art became the epiphanic moment for secular people, the moment that allows them to think that there might be more to this life.

I love the development of painting, where artists work in relationship to the habits of vision that they see in other artists and discover new modalities through which they transform those visions. I understand that E.H. Gombrich's *Art and Illusion* may be far too coherent, but I think Gombrich is right about how artists work in traditions that are always pushing one another. I don't think any artist paints or sculpts to be in a museum. They have to do it *for* somebody. Musicians, composers know that their music is air; the music is not on the page; for it to exist, people have to *hear* it. And many performances may be required before a musician can hear his or her own music.

One of the agonies of being a poet today is, who are you writing for? You have to use the medium you're given, namely, a language in use. You push the envelope of the language in use, make it do more than its everyday use can, and therefore poetry is always happening within the material context. My brand of Marxism really comes out here, because I emphasize the necessary material bases for how lives contribute to one another, and therefore I'm suspicious of art for art's sake. Art for art's sake sounds far too much like art reified within capitalism, something consumed with itself, which therefore cannot resist capitalism. I don't like the modern conceptual art movement, for example—I think it's masturbatory self-involvement, and it drives me crazy. The viewer gets to make it into anything they want to. Well hell, that's just like getting to go shop at Circuit City.

BV: In reading your books, I wasn't aware of how deep your interest in the visual arts is. Now that I know that, I'm wondering if the visual arts are something you might want to explore in your writing.

SH: I don't know how. How do you write about sculpture? Even a picture of a sculpture is not a sculpture. I've often said that you can only act in a world you can see, and you can only see by learning to say. A lot of what I do therefore tries to reclaim the grammar of Christian speech to help us see the world rightly. Now "saying" is not just words, but a kind of shaping that we learn by subjecting ourselves to artistic presentations. This shaping helps us see the world in a way that we never had before, though it was always there to be seen. For that reason, it's important for Christians to be in favor of censorship. Visual art, novels, and poetry can corrupt us, and you should only look at some of it if you've prepared by looking at other things. If you have training within a tradition, you can look at certain kinds of blackness without accepting the blackness on its own terms. I find my life needs beauty. I think the transcendentals are interrelated: truth, goodness, and beauty. And I think our world is ugly. One of the most decisive things you can say about the world capitalism produces is that it's ugly. Therefore I need beauty to give me calm and a continuing critical edge in relationship to the world. We can discover and create zones of beauty to help each other notice the ugliness. An aspect of the moral life is that when you're wrong, when your life isn't going the right directions, you get a sense that it's ugly.

Albert Speer was Hitler's munitions officer and an architect. He was *completely* taken in by Hitler's regime, and of course spent twenty years in Spandau for it. There's a wonderful moment in *Inside the Third Reich*. I think it was in '39. The Nazis were in their victorious mode, and Hitler had sent Speer to Spain to get the Spanish organized. At the Prado, Speer said that for a brief moment he suddenly saw, because of the Prado's simplicity and beauty, that their designs for a thousand-year Reich were ugly. "I could not act on it," he said, "because I was so enmeshed in that life." The Reich *was* ugly. They expected it to fall after a thousand years, and Hitler wanted the ruins to look like ancient Rome, so they designed their buildings with this in mind. A few years ago in Egypt, my wife and I went up the Nile, and when I saw the Temple of Karnak all I could think was that it looked like the Nazis—because they had studied it.

In the context of the ancient Middle and Near East, the anti-iconic aspects of Judaism are fascinating. It is not true that the Jews are anti-art in any way. My colleague Kalman Bland has written a very fine book arguing that the Jews in fact produced all kinds of representational forms of art, but that Christians just didn't notice, and described the Jews as anti-iconic, which the Jews took as a compliment at certain times, though it's not intrinsic to Judaism at all. Israel got onto the fascinating question about representations of God quite early; they had the idea that we can see God in what God is not, but that we should not make God's creation more than just that. They were concerned with this tension in many aspects of life, and we have inherited this. There is a beauty in God's creation that must be performed, but cannot at the same time call attention to itself. I think the Christian practice of representation is at the heart of who we are. It's a constant struggle; representing God is not something you "get right," and then can do over and over in the same way.

BV: Is that tied to John Henry Newman's prayer, where he says, "To the extent that in my dealings with other people they see me and not you,

Lord, it means that I am still opaque and not yet transparent," and that we should be pointing to the cross as opposed to pointing to ourselves?

SH: Yes, but of course pointing to the cross involves an extraordinary intensification of the self. The saints are extraordinarily individuated, yet we see God in that; it's not as if in pointing to the cross you become nothing. A fascinating exercise would be to look at the interrelationship between sainthood and Christian art. To come back for a moment to the subject of Christian humanism, of course Christians should see part of their story in Picasso's *Guernica*, but that doesn't mean that there might not also be something called Christian art. I know that it has become embarrassing for Christians to think that. Christian humanism generally says, art is art, and we Christians don't want to impose anything on art, because that would be puritanical and philistine. But I think there is a beauty that is possible only because of the practices of the Christian community, and I think Christian artists can and should strive for this. Any Christian artist who wants to build up the Christian community will look at the details of the story. For example, I think the centrality of Mary in Christian art is important, and I hope that we continue to produce artists who try to help us see what an extraordinary thing it is, that "Do with me what you will."

You were at church with me on Sunday [Aldersgate]. I have to say that I don't like the space in which I worship, because it's not beautiful. The people are beautiful, and that's good to be forced to recognize—if we had other kinds of beauty around us, I might miss it. But I think we also need beauty on the walls, and we don't have it. We need beauty so that the building itself praises God. We haven't discovered, in our day, a Christian architecture. We haven't produced an architecture denoting a people whom God has made present in the world. The liturgy should also be beautiful, and I think the kinds of experimentation around the liturgy today are not very beautiful.

BV: Have you read von Balthasar?

SH: I've read a good bit and am very sympathetic with the general movement of his thought. I think *Mysterium Paschale* is extraordinary. He sees that the mystery at the heart of the Eucharistic celebration is the kind that produces a beauty that shows, but doesn't say. You might ask how I can say, "shows but doesn't say," since I've claimed that you can only act on a world you can see, and you can only see by learning to say. I'd answer that Christian art is about helping us *see* without explanation. Too often our saying is wordy. We want to describe a cause—as in cause and effect—but there is no explanation of how God shows up in the Eucharist. God is not determined by our understanding of cause and effect.

I think art is really *about* non-violence, and about creation of a world that is attractive. We don't become good by simply *not doing* a lot of things. We become good by being attracted to a world that is so engaging that we can't imagine doing anything else. Cultural formation gives us a way to avoid the violence that we never noticed as violence because it seems so natural.

As I was talking about beauty earlier, I realized that beauty is presumed to be comforting. And I assume beauty also terrorizes. The crucifix is extraordinarily frightening. How to be attracted to the beauty which that terror tails forth—learning that is part of what it means to be a disciple of Jesus.

Stanley Hauerwas: An Interview
Crosscurrents
by Michael J. Quirk

Introduction by Michael J. Quirk:

One often hears the complaint that Stanley M. Hauerwas—Gilbert T. Rowe Professor of Theological Ethics at the Duke University Divinity School, Gifford Lecturer for the year 2001, author of over twenty books and the recently published Hauerwas Reader, and Time magazine's current choice as the "best of" today's theologians—is "difficult to take seriously." In the face of these and other assorted accomplishments and accolades, that charge itself seems hard to take seriously. But Hauerwas often makes it easy for his critics to be dismissive. The theological stands he takes are meticulously argued and thoroughly researched. However the conclusions he reaches seem, to many theologians (whether conservative, liberal, or somewhere in between), to be so over the top that they assume the man must have wandered off the highway of sweet reason somewhere into the thickets of crankdom. Can anyone who enlists folks as different as John Howard Yoder, Pope John Paul II, Stanley Fish, and Michel Foucault in the cause of overcoming modernity and establishing the Church in its place really know what he is doing? Can anyone that cantankerous really be at the same time a serious pacifist? Can anyone as resolutely "traditional" as Hauerwas on the subject of marriage and sexual fidelity not see the contradiction when he quips that "Gays, as a group, are morally superior to Christians, as a group" simply because they have managed to be ostracized by the U.S. military on account of their sexuality? And could anyone seriously think that liberal democracy is all that bad?

This "aw, come off it" dismissiveness seems to me to say more about Hauerwas's critics than Hauerwas himself. For Hauerwas does sweat the details. While his favored form of writing is the short essay rather than the standard-issue scholarly book, his work is scholarly, in the best sense of the word: well-acquainted with the relevant theological literature, and enriched by his proficiency in understanding other genres of writing, such as philosophy, social criticism, and the novel. The craftsmanlike character of his piecework prose (which he attributes, in part, to his earlier apprenticeship as a bricklayer) dares his readership to take him seriously, because he is serious. But to accept that challenge would be to lead one to place in question certain intellectual—and moral—habits that one might find too comforting to give up. Thus Hauerwas suggests that, contrary to the received wisdom, honest fellowship with gays and lesbians may require rather than prohibit loyalty to the virtue of monogamous fidelity, and that pacifism may require that one air one's disagreements publicly and unflinchingly, rather than to try to smooth them over with a false "tolerance" that is more manipulative than it seems on first blush. And, yes, perhaps liberal democracy is all that bad, if it hampers the quest to form good people in decent societies, as Hauerwas insists it does. (It is important to note that for Hauerwas "liberalism" names not just—and not primarily—the politics of those labeled "liberal" in contemporary America, but an entire grand tradition of Western political thought and practice that runs from Hobbes and Locke down to Rawls and Nozick. Contemporary "conservatives" are just as much under fire from his critique as contemporary "liberals." Neither camp can take comfort in his judgments.) In sum, Hauerwas is intentionally disconcerting. That can be an unpleasant experience. Hence, the reluctance, on the part of many theologians and religious scholars, to give him his due.

To give Hauerwas his due is not to say that one must agree with him all the way down the line. This is certainly true in my own case. I have known Stan for the past fourteen years and have carried on a lively and lengthy correspondence with him, through letters and e-mail. Our differences are significant: he is a Pacifist Christian, while I am a "reform Aristotelian" philosopher who adheres to the possibility, if not the likelihood nowadays, of the just war. He believes in the reality of sin; I believe in the dangers of vice. He vouches for the reality of grace, I for the possibility of a virtuous life in trying circumstances. He embraces the Church as the medium of God's lordship in time, I embrace philosophy, and its community of inquiry, as a vocation that makes one's life worthy and worthwhile. (If it was good enough for Socrates, it's good enough for me…) And so on. Even our "insignificant" differences are significant. He is a Texan, I am a New Yorker. He likes the Braves, the Cubs, and the Durham Bulls; I root for the Mets, the Yankees, and the Brooklyn Cyclones (in roughly that order).

Yet I find these differences and disagreements to be incredibly fertile. This is partly due to the fact that to meaningfully disagree with somebody one must share some substantial agreements in common. In particular, I salute Stan's attempt to integrate, into theological reflection, the holism, historicism, and antifoundationalism that has flourished in philosophy for the past few decades: he is well-versed in the ways in which analytic philosophers like Wittgenstein and Kuhn, as well as continentals like Gadamer and Foucault, have challenged the idea of a "universal reason" subsisting apart from particular practices and traditions, and is determined to introduce them, full-strength, into the more nervous precincts of moral theology. As an Aristotelian, I agree with Stan on the need to rehabilitate "thick" conceptions of the virtues of character, as an alternative to the more "thin" notions of obligation that have rendered contemporary versions of Kantianism and Utilitarianism so pale and unconvincing. Finally, I applaud Stan's dogged critique of liberal individualism (and its ugly doppelganger, "late capitalism"), in part because the latter deprives its citizens of any robust opportunities to debate and deliberate on the nature of the good, and in part because the noisy, relentless triumphalism of the liberal-democratic cheerleaders for "globalism" has grown so tiresome, and is so transparently a front for American corporate interests to colonize and homogenize the world.

Yet our disagreements in themselves are just as important: Stan has kept me on my toes over the years, in more ways than I can count. Stan's "outrageousness," when he's not simply telling the truth, has a wonderfully therapeutic quality that goads one not only into examining one's own intellectual commitments (and conscience), but to respond, to the best of one's abilities, in kind. For Stanley, "peace" names the absence of violence, but not of conflict. Indeed it is the cardinal error of political liberalism to think that conflict on important matters can be domesticated, privatized, smoothed over, without losing something very important in the process—namely, a sense of the meaning and worthiness of our lives. Argument does not deny but confirms one's faith in the good will of one's interlocutor: to fail to engage one in argument, when it is not simple squeamishness, is often the grossest sign of disrespect, and a missed opportunity to forge a consensus that might enrich the lives of everyone involved. In this sense, being a Texan like Stan and a being New Yorker like myself are two strangely similar modes of being-in-the-world: both Texas and New York harbor distinctive, strong American regional cultures that thrive on argument, bluntness, and putting one's two cents in. They offer at least the possibility of conflict that is not by definition violence.

What follows is not argument, but conversation—a conversation that centers on Hauerwas's Gifford lectures published by Brazos Press under the title *With the Grain of the Universe*. In this work, Hauerwas reexamines three previous Gifford lecturers—William James, Reinhold Niebuhr, and Karl Barth—from an interesting perspective. Questioning whether "natural theology" as Lord Gifford understood it (i.e., as an entirely "rational" effort beholden to no particular religious tradition) is even intelligible, Hauerwas goes on to reconceive natural theology as something not independent of revelation and tradition, but as the effort of redescribing and reimagining the ways in which Christian faith illuminates and truthfully accounts for the world in which we all live. What results is a fascinating, thought-provoking—and, yes, disturbing—elaboration of the intersection of philosophy and theology in the past century.

* * *

Michael J. Quirk: Your Gifford lectures contain critical appraisals of both William James and Reinhold Niebuhr, as well as the astonishing claim that Karl Barth is the most successful natural theologian of the twentieth century. One usually finds Barth depicted as the resolute enemy of all natural theology. Could you explain how you came to this understanding of Barth?

Stanley Hauerwas: It fits as part of my larger argument that a natural theology is unintelligible separated from a full doctrine of God. And of course what a full doctrine of God entails is an understanding, first of all, that God is not part of the metaphysical furniture of the universe. What many of the Gifford lecturers have assumed is what Nicholas Wolterstorff has called an "evidentialist apologetic" that tried to show that God, as an empty signifier, must exist. And I'm trying to show that if you could successfully show that that God must exist then you would have evidence that the Christian God does not exist, because the Christian God is the God who created gratuitously. So there can be no necessary relationship between creation and God from the Christian point of view. Accordingly, the whole modernist enterprise that the Gifford lectures named was based upon a decisive metaphysical mistake vis-à-vis the Christian doctrine of God. I am also at the same time trying to argue that the Christian doctrine of God requires a corresponding politics. And the corresponding politics is embodied in the necessity of the Church to exist. Of course I relate that also to the necessity of the Jews to exist. I rather like Frederick the Great's response to the question "How do you know God exists?"—"the Jews." I think that is exactly the right kind of answer. But that means that at the same time I am trying to make what might be called a metaphysical argument, I must also develop an ongoing critique of how Christian discourse has been politically privatized in modernity.

MJQ: So, on the metaphysical side of the issue, to put the political aspect aside for the moment, it seems that one of the key texts here must be Barth's essay on St. Anselm's *Proslogion*, where he construes this text not as an independent philosophical proof of the Christian God, but as an explication of that God as God has chosen to reveal himself to the Church. And this cuts across the standard philosophical way of reading Anselm's *fides quaerens intellectum*—that is, of philosophical reason, in and of itself, establishing through *a priori* argument truths about God that revelation also provides, but in a less universal and necessary manner.

SH: Right. Of course it's very important that the story I tell about the Giffords begins with William James, because I want to show that James's account of rationality won't give you a phrase like "reason in and of itself," where reason becomes an autonomous thing that can be made separate from the practices of a community.

MJQ: In other words, James understood that the prevailing self-image of philosophy—as the discipline that supplies, in Leibnizian fashion, the bedrock, universally necessary "truths of reason"—is deceptive, and that any attempt to prove God's existence and nature in that fashion will not work. Doesn't James make a similar mistake, however, to the extent that he replaces the appeal to "reason in and of itself" with radical empiricism, or "experience in and of itself"?

SH: Yeah, that's tricky, though. James sometimes does mistakenly seem to think that experience *qua* experience is an intelligible notion, although I don't develop this line of criticism extensively in my Giffords. But if James followed his own best insights in the *Principles of Psychology*, where he sees that "experience" is the naming of habituation, which is inseparable from forming beliefs, he'd have come off much better.

MJQ: The other possible problem with James is that he doesn't view experience as itself a *political* concept—by which I mean that experience is always experience shaped by certain practices that can themselves be called into question, reaffirmed, or revised by a community that is in pursuit of a determinate vision of the good. James seems, to me at least, to view experience as ultimately just radical experience, not necessarily a function of political practice.

SH: Right. Along similar lines, the other argument I make is that James has no methodological reason to distinguish between experience and what he calls overbeliefs. And his holding on to that distinction in effect just serves to reproduce democratic capitalism's distinction between the public and the private.

MJQ: Could you expand on that a little bit?

SH: James thought, in the *Varieties of Religious Experience*, that the experience *qua* experience of the founders of the various religions really constituted the core of what we later call Judaism, or Christianity, or Hinduism or Buddhism—and everything else was secondhand. These secondary overbeliefs name—and remember James said overbeliefs are the most important things about us—things like God-as-Trinity, which James understood as attempts to go beyond the experience itself. This just strikes me as wrong. I see no reason, on his own understanding of beliefs as habits, for him to take this tack. I read James in an Aristotelian fashion—I don't think he was a voluntarist. "The Will to Believe" is a very Aristotelian text. So I don't think he *should* have distinguished between experience and overbeliefs. I think that distinction came from the continuing influence of Emerson on James—Emerson just thinking that these Christian "doctrines" were just so much balderdash. I have tried to show that James's understanding of Christianity—and really his distaste for it—was not because of his fundamental philosophical views, but because he continued to confuse his philosophical views with an Emersonian account of Christianity—the Emersonian rejection of doctrinal "overbeliefs" as inessential.

MJQ: The other key figure in your narrative, besides Barth and James, is Reinhold Niebuhr. Is the more explicitly Christian, more pessimistic, more "realistic" Niebuhr an advance on James?

SH: No. I hope that the chapters on James will not be overlooked in the overall narrative I tell in the book, because it's very important to see that Niebuhr's account was not as good as James's account. He thought he was borrowing from James, as I show from references to his 1914 B.D. thesis, and he always stayed within James's naturalistic presuppositions about the way things are. He thought that in doing so he was being a pragmatist. But I don't think that Niebuhr ever understood James's claim that truth is something that *happens* to a proposition. Still, he certainly always tried to stay within a kind of Jamesian framework, so Christianity becomes "powerful symbols" that give you a provocative account of "the human condition."

MJQ: So would you think it fair to say that in Niebuhr James's political chickens come home to roost—that James's account of radical experience was empty enough to be filled with a "political realism" of which James himself would likely disapprove?

SH: Right. What's really crucial for me about Niebuhr is that he represents what I regard, in another essay I wrote some time ago, as "the democratic policing of Christianity." Democracy in James was a rather vague set of notions, never really worked out in any institutionalized sense. Niebuhr's account viewed democracy as equally vague, but you can see that, because of his strong political realism, Christianity was, in a determinative way, political for Niebuhr. In Niebuhr you get Christianity commended primarily as what's very, very good for the kind of realism that you need to sustain a democratic social order. And so I really am serious when I claim that Christianity has died as a result of its love affair with liberal democracy. I think that liberal democracy, in many ways, took as its fundamental task to kill Christianity by domesticating its strongest views. And it's done that! I'm not mad at liberals, in any way, for that. I get angry at Christians for their failure to see that that's what's been happening to us for the last two hundred years.

MJQ: If that's the case, then it's not particularly clear what Christians need to do other than just hang together as Christians. And how does that work itself out in practical terms? For instance, a recent article in *Commonweal* by Eugene McCarraher on "Radical Orthodoxy" expressed broad sympathy toward its critique of liberal capitalist democracies, but lamented its lack of concrete proposals as to how to live out the full-strength Christianity it advocates. Since you share with the Radical Orthodoxy group the conviction that Christians blew it regarding liberal democracy, what ought Christians to do, as opposed to merely *think* or *believe*?

SH: Well, first of all, what you do is quit trying to *save* liberal democracy. Don't let your imaginations be seized by "public policy issues." "Public policy issues" is always conservative politics within a liberal democratic regime. I am very sympathetic with people in the C. B. MacPherson school of political theory—people like Peter Euben, Ronald Beiner, and Jean Bethke Elshtain—who have seen how liberal democracy, particularly exemplified in people like Rawls, is really the end of politics. Because, in a funny way, liberalism doesn't want to deal with the conflict that is necessarily part of the political.

MJQ: Meaning that it wants to steer conflict into those issues that prescind from any "thick conception of the good," seeking to establish some "thin" conception of the good as the limiting framework for political argument and deliberation? But the problem here, as I see it, is that you can't have a thin conception without presupposing a thick conception to begin with.

SH: Right. And so I am not unsympathetic with those who are trying to develop some accounts of deliberative [as opposed to procedural] democracy. But then when you start thinking about deliberative democracy what I'm always curious about is, institutionally, where can that be found? It sure as hell can't be found in Washington, D.C. I think of it as at home, for example, among members of Aldersgate United Methodist Church, when we have to make decisions about our new pastor's housing and the like. We have a Pastoral Staff Relations Committee where we hammer all that out. *That's* deliberative democracy! You really are trying to make concrete decisions in the light of a good that the community names. Namely: we need pastoral leadership for the right administration of the sacraments and the good preaching of the word. That's *real* politics!

MJQ: Interestingly, this seems to be John Dewey's conception of democracy, especially in light of his critique of what he called the "old" liberalism—an individualistic, procedural doctrine that left deliberation of "ends" to the "private" sphere. If I am hearing you correctly, you're saying that folks like Dewey were looking in the wrong place for democracy. You won't find it in legislatures or polling places. You're more likely to find it in, say, the National Conference of Catholic Bishops debating war or the economy, or Torah scholars debating the fine points of the Law, than in the secular politics of the nation-state. Quite an irony for Dewey, the unabashed secularist.

SH: Yes. And Dewey had such a high regard for social science. Now there's nothing about Dewey that's stupid, but I do think that his understanding of the moral character of the social sciences has proven very hard to sustain within the regimes of knowledges in the modern university. Social science now becomes "rational choice methodology."

MJQ: Which is something that would've given Dewey the creeps.

SH: I can't believe that he wouldn't have gone berserk. Because "rational choice methodology" is just the institutionalization of capitalist exchange models now seen as "explaining" every form of human relations. But it gives a kind of predictability that social sciences so desire to make them seem "scientific."

MJQ: As long as we are on the subject of democracy, Jeffrey Stout, in a new edition of *Ethics After Babel*, has argued that your critique of that book betrays antidemocratic sympathies. Could you respond to this charge?

SH: Jeff wants democracy to be a kind of Whitmanesque democratic expression. And I have to say that I'm not terribly impressed with self-expression. I know that Whitman has "brotherhood" as well, but I think there is a deep tension between those expressive modes of philosophical psychology associated with those accounts and any attempt at naming goods that I think are crucial to any genuine deliberative body. Basically, I think Jeff is mad at MacIntyre and myself because we don't like what he likes. He thinks we're sloppy—well, he thinks *I'm* sloppy, not necessarily Alasdair—about words like "justice." But I *don't* think that "justice" is a straight-up virtue. I think it's dependent upon more determinative notions of the good. Because I don't want "justice" becoming the all-determining virtue—and of course the way liberals handle "justice" it isn't even a virtue—that determines the content of all the other virtues. I am classically Aristotelian on this score.

MJQ: I know what you mean. The chapter on justice in the *Nicomachean Ethics*, if you read it out of context apart from Aristotle's treatment of all the other virtues, makes no sense at all. It seems to be a mixture of obscure pronouncements on "proportion" in distribution and retribution, coupled with platitudes about "giving each his or her due." Yet the *goods* that justice must secure are described in detail in his treatment of the other virtues and their constitutive role in the common good of the *polis*. Read *in* context, his account of justice makes perfect sense.

SH: That's right. But political liberals assume that the primary political task is to secure cooperative agreement between people who share nothing in common other than the fear of death. And they call that cooperative agreement "justice," which derives from the necessity of our respecting one another, for the very achievement of those kinds of cooperative agreements. I just think that such an account already envisions a social order that is less than good, because it doesn't produce good people. Such an account becomes peculiarly problematic within a capitalist economy, in which "justice" names the pursuit of interests without any determination of the content of those interests.

MJQ: It seems to me that both liberal theologians and conservative theologians don't "get" you. The liberals tend to read you as one who rejects the liberatory potential of Christianity and withdraws into a kind of pietistic sect, and will not "get real" and engage the world, especially the political world, on its own terms in such a way that "Christ transforms culture." For their part, the conservatives (e.g., quite a few *First Things* articles on you) cannot see how you can coherently combine your orthodox views on, say, the trinity or Christology with the antifoundationalist, postmodern, Stanley-Fish-esque stuff, not to mention your views on, say, gays, war, capitalism, the United States of America, etc. In fact, on some of the latter issues, you seem a lot closer to left-wing radicals like Noam Chomsky, while on others you seem close to "paleoconservatives" like Robert Nisbet, without the former's dogmatic secularism and the latter's Burkean views on tradition and the sacredness of nation. I would like to know how you react to this curious lack of understanding.

SH: I think the theological liberals are *right* to hate me, because I represent for them a recovery of unapologetic Christian speech that's doing work. I have tried to name the politics that is necessary for it to do work, and it's not their politics. Theological liberalism is Protestant pietism gone to seed. Basically, the theological liberals think that every individual needs some kind of determinative relationship with God which they *might* find expressed in a communal body called the Church, *maybe*. And of course I'm just thoroughly Catholic in this regard. I think salvation is necessarily mediated across time by a body of people, and if you don't have that body of people then you don't have that salvation. So there's just some very sharp differences between myself and what I regard as the project of Protestant liberal theology. The latter wanted to show that you could redescribe the Christian faith in languages that make it sound like you're still talking about what Christians talked about in the past but in fact you're not. And Reinhold Niebuhr is of course the classic example of that.

MJQ: Despite his reputation of being neo-orthodox?

SH: Yes—you know, the whole point of how he was fond of quoting the London *Times* that original sin was the only Christian doctrine that was empirically verifiable. Well that's false. "Original Sin" is not a description of something called "the human condition."

MJQ: To say that "people tend to be bad" is not the same as endorsing the doctrine of original sin...

SH: Not at all. If we're shits, we're shits: that's not the same thing as saying we're sinners. I mean, you cannot have sin without the Christian understanding of God, or the Jewish understanding of God.

MJQ: So much for theological liberals. How about the conservatives?

SH: The conservatives, I think, continue to let their views about Christian salvation be policed by their democratic presuppositions. And so they want to have their Jesus without the implications, for example, for living nonviolently. And I just don't think you can do that. And philosophically, as far as I'm concerned, they just don't get it. When they hear me, they keep saying "Well how do you defeat relativism?" They assume if you don't have a theory about how you defeat relativism, then the Nazis are around the corner.

MJQ: It's as if Wittgenstein or Gadamer never existed...

SH: Exactly. And I want to say, Look, where you go wrong is beginning to think that you *know* what relativism is, which you then need to defeat.

MJQ: Or that to defeat the relativist, or the Nazi, they think you need...

SH: They think you need a *theory*! That's absolutely crazy. And what's interesting is that those philosophical moves have extraordinary theological implications. If you say you need a theory to know if it might be true that God raised Jesus from the dead, worship that *theory*, don't worship the crucified and risen Jesus. So in an odd way, philosophical commitments that aim to defeat something called relativism can lead very quickly to a reductionistic Christology. Which theological conservatives don't *do* because they somehow keep the Christology "in church." I don't want to just keep it "in church."

MJQ: Your mention of "relativism" and the various philosophical responses to it brings to mind a very different intellectual figure, Richard Rorty. There are curious points of contact between your own project and his. Both of you are antifoundationalists, both of you reject the idea that knowledge needs to be grounded in truths that are immediately available to all rational beings, both of you acknowledge the historicity of all theory and practice. But Rorty is an atheist—in fact, a nononsense atheist who has no patience with those who want to make religious claims palatable to unbelievers—and you are Christian. Rorty thinks that his atheism naturally flows from the sort of antifoundationalist, historicist attitude that characterizes his philosophy, and you think that Christianity is the most historicist, antifoundationalist system of belief and practice there is. Moreover, Rorty is a liberal who has endeavored to show that nonfoundational, indeed un-philosophical liberalism is the politics that best fits his kind of philosophy, and you are an antiliberal who claims that any form of liberalism will not fit this kind of philosophy, or in your case, theology. How would you account for these differences?

SH: I don't think my antifoundationalism is altogether the same as Rorty's. People have confused having antifoundationalist views with also being a kind of linguistic idealist, and I am not—I am a Wittgensteinian realist. Rorty may be too, in that respect, but it's not quite clear that he is. But I think the deepest disagreement between myself and Rorty is, as with Stout, that he likes what I dislike. Rorty wants to destroy Christianity. I like his candor in that respect. I'm always interested, though, in what parts of Christianity atheists like Rorty want to continue.

MJQ: Rorty has unapologetically described himself as a *"freeloading"* atheist with respect to Christianity. That seems to me to suggest an extraordinarily ahistorical way for a professed historicist to deal with Christianity—as if it were a menu of moral items from which one can pick and choose without fear of incoherence. That you can junk Trinitarianism and Christology but still hold on to the Sermon on the Mount...

SH: Yeah, he wants that as politics but he hates, of course, Christian concerns about abortion. I don't know where he stands on marriage or monogamous fidelity. He certainly doesn't like any of the sexual ethics that might complicate how to think about gay relationships and so on. That's just, as far as he is concerned.

MJQ: Just private stuff.

SH: Private stuff left over from a bad time, and we'll slowly outgrow all that. Still, I love to read Rorty. I like his imagination and candor. Rorty just thinks that Christianity is false. Where, on his own philosophical grounds, he gets that kind of certainty, is an interesting question.

MJQ: I want to conclude with a question that is of tremendous

eschatological importance, and that you are uniquely qualified to answer: Will there ever be another Yankees-Mets subway series before the end of time?
SH: No! No! Never again!

Sundries

On Being a Theologian:
Remarks on Receiving an Honorary Doctorate from Marymount Manhattan College

President Shaver, graduates, families and friends of the graduates, I must begin with a confession. I think it best to make a clean breast of things just to make sure you understand what you are doing by giving me this honorary degree. I do not want you embarrassed by having what I must confess later revealed. I realize that what I have to reveal may be particularly offensive for New Yorkers. I am an Atlanta Braves fan. I cannot tell you how painful it is to watch Tommy Glavine pitch for the New York Mets. Of course, things could be worse—Tommy could be pitching for the Yankees. At least the Mets are in the National League where baseball is still played. Everyone knows that the designated batter is the end of baseball as we knew it.

Yet, I have to acknowledge that the Yankees have had some extraordinary players—in particular, everyone's favorite, Lou Gehrig. Gehrig was not only one of the greatest players to play the game, but in the words of Sam Jones—Sam Jones being a pitcher for Cleveland and Boston who for five years never threw to first base to hold a runner, and when he finally did throw to first base he had the runner out by a mile, but, unfortunately, his first baseman was so surprised he dropped the ball—Jones says, Gehrig was "One of the nicest fellows ever lived. He never really got the publicity he deserved. A very serious-minded fellow, very modest and easy to get along with, every inch a gentleman."

Gehrig, moreover, made the greatest speech a baseball player has ever made. Beset by an illness from which he would soon die, when he retired he said simply, "I am the luckiest man alive."

I am not suffering from an illness (as long as we do not count life itself as an illness) that implies my imminent death, but like Gehrig, I believe I am among the luckiest of people. I am extremely fortunate to be honored by you today, but this wonderful acknowledgement by you is not why I think that I am so lucky. I also have a wonderful wife and family, but neither are they the reason, at least on this occasion, I think myself so lucky. Rather, I think of myself as the luckiest man alive because, like Lou Gehrig, everyday I get to do what I love, that is, to be a theologian in the church of Jesus Christ.

I realize that some of you may find that rather strange. Baseball is one thing. Theology is quite another. Almost all of us, men and women alike, dream at some time in our lives of being in the major leagues. Indeed, it was only when I was in my late forties and had injured my rotator cuff that I realized my major league potential was probably lost forever. Few dream of being a theologian. The truth of the matter is that I do not ever remember wanting to be a theologian. I began the trek through divinity and graduate school just trying to figure out (Texans "figure out") what all this Christian stuff was about, but somewhere along the way, I realized, as strange and weird as it may seem, that I had become a theologian. Not only had I become a theologian, but also theology was an activity, a good and compelling work, that I could no longer not do.

That anyone can gain that kind of satisfaction from the study of theology can be problematic from a theological point of view. After all, you need to remember that the subject of theology is God. God, moreover, is not your everyday academic subject. If you think that you are beginning to understand something about God, that is an indication that you have probably made a deep mistake. For example, Rowan Greer, in his book *Christian Hope and Christian Life*, prefaces his remarks concerning the contribution of Gregory of Nyssa to debates surrounding the Trinity with the observation that it is important "to recognize that the people who first clarified the Christian doctrine of the Trinity were committed to the doctrine that God is incomprehensible." Yet, Christians believe that this same incomprehensible God refuses to let our sin deter God's determination to befriend us. I hope, therefore, that it is not surprising that some of us find a deep satisfaction that the church has called us to be theologians. It is extremely important, however, that those of us so called never forget that the office of theology is one of the minor offices of the church.

Another reason it may seem a bit odd to gain such satisfaction from being a theologian is that doing theology can get you into a lot of trouble. Certainly, I have gotten into a lot of trouble. Some think that this has less to do with my being a theologian and more to do with the fact that I am just an "ornery" Texan. It would only be an invitation to self-deception for me to try to separate the one from the other, but I do think, particularly in our day, that it does not take much theological insight to get you in trouble. For example, just think about the reaction to the commonplace theological observation that pride is a sin—including the pride expressed by many, particularly after September 11, in being American.

About the worst thing you can do about pride, especially the pride in "Proud to be an American," is try to will your way out of it. God's alternative to pride is called friendship. By making us friends with one another through the Eucharist, we are unselfed, and we discover that pride of country must be qualified by the deeper unity the church makes possible. It is important that we not forget that Christians had a word to describe what some mean by "globalization" long before that word came along. The Christian word was, and remains, "catholic."

I am honored by the honor you have given me this wonderful day, a wonderful day in particular for those of you who are graduating. I congratulate you. I am honored that I have some role in your graduation ceremony. It gives me particular delight to be recognized by a school like Marymount Manhattan College. Whatever good I may have done would not have been possible without the support and formation I have been given by Catholic friends, the Catholic Church, and Catholic institutions.

So, to receive this degree from Marymount Manhattan means a great deal to me. But, I hope that I am able to remember that even as I receive this gift I have already received more than I could ever have desired just to the extent that God somehow, and surely only God can know how, gave me the good work to do called theology.

Explaining Why Willimon Never Explains

1. Blowing Willimon's Cover

Will Willimon is one of the least obvious people I have ever known. He is very good at being less than obvious. He appears to be such a nice guy. He wants everyone to like him. He has self- deprecating irony down to a fine art. Indeed, I think Will is one of the best practitioners of the Southern Con I have ever known. The Southern Con is usually perfected by Southerners who have had to live for a time in that mythic place called, "The North." I do not know if Will perfected his use of the Southern Con while he was at Yale, but he is a paradigmatic example of this extremely useful strategy.

The Southern Con can take many different forms, but there is a common structure to the way it works. It goes something like this: "I'm just a good ol' boy from the red dirt of South Carolina so I do not have your sophistication. Indeed, I am not even sure I know what the word sophistication means. But if I heard you right it seems to me that . . .." The dots represent the Southern Con artist use of a quote from Plato or Dylan Thomas that subverts his or her interlocutor's position. Of course, such con artists pretend they do not know it is a quote from Plato or Dylan Thomas, but you had better believe they know what they are doing when they express their "ignorance." Southerners suspect that Paul must have had some proleptic training in being a Southerner because his speech to the Athenians in Acts 17 is a paradigmatic example of the Southern Con.

Even though I'm not from the "South" (Texans simply do not have the passive-aggressive tendencies Southerners confuse with charm), I admire Will's use of the Southern Con. He uses the strategy of the Southern Con to hide his extraordinary reading habits as well as his intellectual depth. Will Willimon—no matter how many times he tells you he is just another Methodist preacher—is an exceptionally smart guy. I will use this occasion, therefore, to expose the metaphysical presumptions that inform Will's preaching and his understanding of pastoral theology.[19] I will explain why Will never explains and why his refusal to provide explanations is so important for those who would and should imitate him.

Before I take up the task of explaining why Will never explains, however, I need to call attention to some of the other less than obvious aspects of Will's character and work. One of the aspects of Will's life that can be missed is his extraordinary love of the Methodist Church. I could not understand, for example, why Will would have ever "wanted" to be a bishop. I counseled him not to let his name go forward. I pointed out that if he was elected bishop he would have to spend the rest of his life dealing with mediocre guys who expressed their frustration with the ministry by sleeping with the wrong person, but he was undeterred. I think that the only explanation you can give for why he would go through the demeaning exercise the Methodists call "electing a bishop" is that he really loves the Methodist church. One of the things that I love about Will is that he not only loves the Methodist church, but he loves the differences he often finds in and between the denominations before whom he speaks. Will is a critic of the church, but his criticisms are those only a lover could produce.

Will is also quite adept at hiding the fact that he is intellectual. He loves ideas. He seems so "people" oriented, he is "pastoral," but I know of few people who read as much as Will. He not only loves to read, but he also loves to read in areas about which he knows almost nothing. That means Will is not an academic. Will is far too undisciplined (and I mean the description "undisciplined" to be a compliment) to be an academic. This is why he is such a good Dean of the Chapel at Duke. There is almost nothing in which he is not interested. As a result, his sermons and

---

[19] For my understanding of these matters as "metaphysical" see my chapter, "Connections Created and Contingent: Aquinas, Preller, Wittgenstein, and Hopkins" in my *Performing the Faith: Bonhoeffer and The Practice of Nonviolence* (Grand Rapids: Brazos Press, 2004).

his books are filled with wonderful surprises. Surprises that make hearing and reading him such a pleasure.

Finally, I think it is not at all obvious that Will, as the title of this book suggests, is a prophet.[20] Will may be a prophet, even a "peculiar prophet," but I suspect that description embarrasses him. I am often introduced as a prophet and I know I am embarrassed to be so described. No one making as much money as Will and I make, as compromised by our positions in the contemporary university as we are, as culturally accommodated as we are, should be described as a prophet. We both get too much pleasure out of what we do to be so described. Prophets usually have to be forced to be prophets. Prophets do not find their calling fun. Yet, Will is filled with fun, which is one of the attractive aspects of his ministry. At the very least prophets are usually only rightly identified retrospectively.

I make this observation about Will as a prophet to suggest that one of the other less obvious aspects of Will's character is his genuine modesty. He is so, I suspect, because he is constantly surprised that he is getting away with what he is getting away with. I recognize his surprise, because I look upon my own life in quite a similar fashion. Will and I do not come from "high cotton" families or cultures. We live in fear that someone will stand up after we have spoken and ask, "You really do not know what you are talking about, do you?" We will have to acknowledge that we really do not know what we are talking about, but we are determined to say what we think necessary anyway. Will is determined to say what he thinks needs to be said because he is possessed by a passion for the Gospel. Yet, the same passion that makes him go where only fools would go also makes Will modest. How could it be otherwise, given the Gospel he must preach week after week?

I hope that in these few remarks about Will's character I have "blown his cover." He is one of the least obvious people I have ever known. That he is so, I think, has everything to do with why he is rightly seen as one of our best preachers. He is not conned by his use of the Southern Con, which means that his sermons and his pastoral theology display an honesty that we desperately need. I have no doubt that is why so many look to him as an exemplary preacher and pastor.

---

[20]The reference is to William Malamberi and Michael Turner, eds., *Peculiar Prophet: Will Willimon and the Art of Preaching* (Nashville: Abingdon Press, 2004).

Sundries

2. Why Willimon Never Explains

Will Willimon has less philosophical ability than anyone I have ever met. Will likes to tell the story that in his first course in philosophy in college the instructor asked him to sit in the back of the room and, in effect, color in his coloring book. The instructor did so after Will had tried, day in and day out, to ask questions. There is just something about philosophy that Will does not get. I do not mean it to be a compliment that he does not "get philosophy," but I do think his lack of philosophical ability is one of the reasons he is such a good preacher. Let me explain why Will does not explain.

One of the remarkable things about Will's sermons is that he does not try to help us to understand what is "really going on" in the text. He does not try to explain the passage from Scripture because he does not think the text is really about "something else." In other words, he does not assume that there is a depth we need to discover that is more important than the text itself. The assumption by many that such a depth is "there" or needs to be "there" is often the result of philosophical training of which Will is happily innocent. Some of us were only able to get over our philosophical hunger for "depth" through the extensive therapy provided by Wittgenstein. Will did not need Wittgenstein, because he had never been seduced by the philosophical need that many assume can only be satisfied by something deeper. That something deeper is often thought to be a "theory."

At least, during the time I have been listening to Will's sermons, he has never invited his hearers to find something more basic or important than the stories we find in the Scripture. Some of his most memorable sermons are those with one or two word titles such as "More," "Here," or his memorable Easter sermon, "He's Back."[21] In those sermons, Willimon works to free us from our narcissistic desire to find some meaning in the text relevant to our lives. He reminds us that the "meaning" just is what the text helps us to understand about the God who would show up as Jesus.

---

[21] The sermons "More" and "Here" can be found in our book, *Preaching to Strangers* (Louisville: Westminster/John Knox Press, 1992), pp. 113-134. I do not know if "He's Back" has ever been published.

Disrupting Time

Let me try to illustrate how I think Willimon works by providing an example I often use. When I was in seminary I saw the film, "The Servant," which featured the great English actor, Dirk Bogarde. The film tells the story of the second son of an entitled and wealthy British family who has come back to England after serving in the army in India. (Second sons had to serve in the army because they were second sons.) The film takes place in England some time in the early twentieth century at the height of British imperial power. Returning home, the young man realizes he needs "a man servant," because he is, after all, from the English upper classes and accordingly has no sense of how to get through life. Dirk Bogarde plays the servant who is hired to help this young man to reintegrate himself into upper class society.

Bogarde does all that is expected, teaching his master what clothes to wear, what club he ought to join, who his friends should be, and what to eat at a restaurant. The young man quickly becomes quite a success. In the process of helping his master become a "gentleman," however, the servant introduces the young man to gambling, the use of drugs, and to the use of women who are willing to sell sexual favors to men. The servant does so because such behavior is thought to be what unattached English gentlemen do. By the end of the movie, however, the young man has squandered his wealth, become a hopeless drug addict, and is being arrested for killing a woman he had been involved with sexually. In the last scene of the movie in which his master is arrested, the servant—who we now understand has planned the destruction of the one he serves from the beginning—simply walks away.

What is fascinating about this movie is that no explanation is given for the servant's project for destroying his master. No suggestions about the servant's motivations are made in the movie. You simply watch the servant leading the young man to his destruction. Leaving the theater (I have seen the film several times) you hear people say to one another, "Proletarian revenge," or "A clear case of repressed homosexuality." The film leaves you desperate for an explanation, but it gives you no explanation, so the viewer must supply one. Yet, I think the film is trying to suggest that is exactly what you should not do, because there is no explanation for evil.

I often have used this example to suggest to my students why the "story of the fall" in the book of Genesis takes the form of a story. The story does not explain how sin came into the world. The story cannot explain how sin came into the world, because there can be no explanation for why sin came into the world. Sin should not exist, but it does. Barth rightly calls sin an "ontological impossibility" in order to indicate that sin quite simply is absurd.[22] Indeed, it is a mistake to think that the description "sin" explains human evil. Sin is not an explanation of something deeper. Sin, given the story of the Bible, is a description of that for which no other description will do.

In like manner, "creation" does not explain our existence, but rather is a description required by our faith that we are created. To ask why there is something rather than nothing may be an interesting exercise for the philosophically minded. I suspect, however, that those who seek to use the question to try to convince others that they must believe in a god because "something must have started it all" is a mistake. God is not an explanation for our existence. Rather, God is the name we have been given to address the one alone who is worthy of worship. That Christians believe God is the Father, the Son, and the Holy Spirit is but the discovery of the church we believe made possible and necessary by the death and resurrection of Christ and the work of the Spirit at Pentecost. That we learn to address God as Trinity does not mean, however, that we are explaining God.

I believe that nothing more characterizes Will's preaching than his respect for the language, the vocabulary, of the faith as a grammar of description. His sermons are the ongoing attempt to help himself and his hearers learn the grammar of the faith by learning when they have said all that can be said. I have no idea from whom or how Willimon learned to so preach, but I certainly think all the reading he has done in Barth over the years could not have hurt. The very character of Barth's *Dogmatics* is shaped by Barth's fundamental conviction that you cannot explain the Christian faith. Attempts to "explain" are just another name for Protestant liberalism. Barth left explanation behind because he recognized that if God is God we cannot explain on grounds other than God's revelation who God is. Barth quite wonderfully imitates the character of the Bible by refusing to say more than can be said. I think that the irresistible

---

[22] For Barth's most extensive discussion of sin, see *Church Dogmatics* IV/1, trans. G. W. Bromiley (New York: Scribner's Sons, 1956), 157-513.

temptation for some to try to write "a life of Jesus" is fueled by the Gospels' reticence to elaborate on Jesus' life. We want to know more about what it must have meant for Jesus to grow up, but we are told so little. "And Jesus increased in wisdom and in years, and in divine and human favor" (Luke 2:52). That is all we are going to get. The Gnostic gospels cannot resist telling us more about his childhood, and of course, that is why they are Gnostic gospels. Gnosticism in its many forms is but the temptation to know more than is needed.

Will's sermons are his way of trying to help us resist the temptation to explain. We are not to speculate about what "must have really been going on" in Jesus' self-consciousness. Attempts to discern what Jesus must have been thinking in this or that circumstance fail to be disciplined by the silence of Scripture. Not only do attempts to "figure Jesus out" presuppose a quite misleading philosophical psychology, but they are sinful just to the extent that such attempts represent our attempt to make the Gospel fulfill our desires. The "search for the historical Jesus," I fear, too often is but a symptom of our pride, a pride, moreover, that refuses to be humbled by the invitation to be a disciple. We try to substitute "trying to understand" for what it means to follow Jesus.

In *Preaching to Strangers* I criticized Will for sometimes reproducing in his sermons what Lindbeck described as the "experimental-expressive" account of religious conviction.[23] I noted that, given the context of Duke Chapel in which you are basically preaching to strangers, it is very hard to avoid that strategy. However, I think Will's refusal to explain is a very effective mode of resistance to our endemic desire to make Jesus fit into our lives. To so preach risks "not being relevant to the real needs of people," but the whole point is to have our "real needs" transformed. Will's sermons, I believe, represent his attempt to provide us with reminders that no explanation is required because it is not "all about us."

Will's refusal to explain is the reason he also refuses to "translate" the Gospel into other registers such as existentialism, moral lessons, or psychological insights. Words matter for Will. So, like the poet, he cannot try to explain the poem in words the poem does not use. Rather, he must try to help us understand why it *has* to be in these words and not others.

---

[23]See my "Introduction" to *Preaching to Strangers*, 1-15.

Of course, he has to use other words to help us understand why these words matter, but that is why preaching remains an art—an art that like all art is disciplined by imitating past and present masters.

That Will never explains helps explain why he is not afraid to be repetitious. In *With the Grain of the Universe*, I call attention to Barth's claim that "we can only repeat ourselves."[24] Barth could only repeat himself because he rightly understood that theology cannot be some position deeper than Scripture itself, but theology must be a witness to Scripture's witness to God's word. So understood, theology is the attempt to assemble reminders that help us focus our attention on God.[25] The sermon is God's word just to the extent that the word does not replace the Word witnessed in Scripture.

Will, moreover, is a master of repetition. Some may get tired of his use of Gladys, but the telling story matters. Will has the impressive ability to tell the right story at the right time. His stories rarely illustrate a more basic point. Rather his stories are the point, which means that he must often tell the story without saying why he is telling the story. Either the story "works" or it does not. Will, therefore, must risk that his hearers will not "get" the story, but that is why he has to tell it again. The church calls the necessity to tell the story again and again "preaching." Will never explains because he is a preacher.

3. Then Why Is Will So Popular?

If I am right about Willimon's refusal to explain, how do we account for his popularity? "Popularity" may be the wrong word, but at the very least some account needs to be given of why Will is in such demand as a preacher and lecturer. That he is one of the least obvious persons I know may account for why many find what Will does so compelling. That this good old boy from South Carolina has such interesting things to say is a

---

[24]Stanley Hauerwas, *With the Grain of the Universe: The Church's Witness and Natural Theology* (Grand Rapids: Brazos Press, 2001), 173-184.
[25]In *The Spirit of Early Christian Thought* (New Haven: Yale University Press, 2003), Robert Wilken observes that when Augustine wrote about the Trinity he was not seeking "a theological concept or an explanation as such, but the living God who is Father, Son, and Holy Spirit, the 'Trinity that is God, the true and supreme and only God'" (108).

mystery that attracts our interest. Of course, one of the reasons, I suspect, that many find Will intriguing is he does have something to say. In a world that is drowning in platitudes, hearing someone with something to say feels very much like discovering a wonderful land in the midst of a vast and unchartered ocean.

I often observe that Will is such a great preacher because he is an exemplary Southern story teller. Southern story tellers have never let the truth get in the way of telling a good story. Will is a collector of good stories that he makes more than they are by using one story to tell another story. To use one story to tell another story, of course, is a description of how the Bible works. The Bible is the story of the beginning and the end that requires stories that never end except in another story. That is why preaching can never come to an end and why Will—who by disposition always wants to tell you another story—is such a great preacher.

Will is a great preacher because he helps us see the connections. When you cannot explain, you begin to realize the work of preaching and theology is finding the connections between the stories. The Bible is an anthology of wildly different stories, and it is not immediately apparent how they interrelate. Preaching, and the theology that serves preaching, is the ongoing exploration of the church to discover the connections. Christian doctrine is the hints the church has discovered that help us see the connections. The connections are made through the discoveries that the stories not only make possible but also demand.[26]

That Will always wants to tell you another story is, therefore, one reason he is in such high demand as a preacher. Theologically, he is committed to not being apologetic, which makes him a compelling

---

[26]Robert Wilken observes, "The Scriptures are the 'ground and pillar of our faith,' says Irenaeus. If the Bible is dismembered to serve an exotic theological program and biblical texts are deployed willy-nilly (as the Gnostics did), the Scriptures will remain a closed book and it will not be possible 'to find the truth in them.' Without a grasp of the plot that holds everything together, the Bible is as vacuous as a mosaic in which the tiles have been arbitrarily rearranged without reference to the original design or as a poem constructed by stringing together random verses from the *Iliad* and *Odyssey* and imagining it was Homer. . . . Whether one reads Athanasius against Arius, Augustine against Pelagius, or Cyril of Alexandria against Nestorius, all assume that individual passages are to be read in the light of the story that gives meaning to the whole." *The Spirit of Early Christian Thought*, 67-68.

Christian apologist. I think he is so because, as I have argued, he refuses to explain. By refusing to explain, he invites us into a world otherwise unimaginable, and we are fascinated and intrigued. We are fascinated and intrigued because the world called the Gospel is at once so beautiful and so dangerous. We fear danger, but Will helps us see that without the beauty and danger of the Gospel we are condemned to lives of boredom.

I should like to think, moreover, that one of the things Will and I share in common is that neither of us can stand boredom. I hope our disdain for the boring is not because we need constant highs to sustain our lives. Actually, we both live lives that I suspect most people would find boring. After all, we spend most of our time reading and writing—not exactly most people's idea of what it might mean to live an exciting life. What hopefully excites us, however, is that we find it extraordinary that God can make use of people as uninteresting as ourselves. God is great. That Will never fails to remind us that God is great I believe to be one of the reasons so many find his preaching so compelling. Yet, who am I to explain the work of the Spirit?

Confessions of a Mennonite Camp Follower

1. Getting to Know You, Getting To Know All About You[27]

I am aware that I have a certain reputation among the Mennonites. I felt honored that Craig Haas and Steve Nolt in their book *The Mennonite Starter Kit: A Handy Guide for the New Mennonite* included me in the list of "Non-Mennonites Whom Mennonites Wish Were Mennonites."[28] Since theirs is the most incisive book on contemporary Mennonite life, I clearly have been given a status I cannot pretend to deserve. It does give me pause, of course, that the list also includes Lloyd Bentsen (from Texas?), Rembrandt (catering no doubt to Mennonites' pretension that they care about art), Thomas Muentzer (they have to be kidding!), Ronald Reagan, and Alice Parker (who is Alice Parker?). So I am extremely pleased to have been asked to contribute to this issue of the *Mennonite Quarterly Review* on how my "thought" has been shaped by an engagement with Radical Reformation theology.

My initial encounter with the Mennonites did not go well. Growing up in Texas, I had never heard of the Mennonites. If I knew one or two, they did not make themselves known to me as Mennonites. I learned nothing about Mennonites at Southwestern University in Georgetown, Texas. They may have been mentioned in some history or religion course,

---

[27]To be sung as if Julie Andrews were a Mennonite.
[28]Craig Haas and Steve Nolt, *The Mennonite Starter Kit: A Handy Guide For The New Mennonite* (Intercourse PA: Good Books, 1993), 12.

but I do not remember it. I must have read about Mennonites in Williston Walker's *A History of the Christian Church*, but whatever I read made no impression.[29] Only when I ran into actual Mennonites did I realize that there was something different about them—and I did not like the difference.

The first Mennonite I ever knew must have been Mel Schmidt, who appeared during my second or third year in seminary. He and his wife lived in married student housing, where we became acquainted. I vaguely remember that Mel withheld his taxes, or at least we had a discussion about tax withholding. Vietnam had not yet become the "event" that made tax resistance the "thing to do." All I remember is that I thought it very strange that anyone would do anything that radical. Years later Mel and I recalled my stupidity when I gave a lecture at Bluffton, Ohio when Mel was pastor at Bluffton Mennonite.

However, the encounter with a Mennonite that I remember in some detail occurred in 1966 or 1967, during a trip to Harvard for a joint colloquium of Harvard and Yale graduate students in ethics. By this time the Vietnam war was the subject for endless discussions. In the car on the way to Cambridge we were debating whether or not the war was just. In the course of the discussion a new and very quiet graduate student made judgments that suggested he might be a pacifist. He even mentioned John Howard Yoder, of whom, of course, none of us had ever heard. I was shocked that the Yale Graduate School would actually accept anyone so naive. I, of course, tried to intimidate him, using Niebuhrian arguments. His name was Leroy Walters, and he is now the distinguished ethicist at the Kennedy Center for Bioethics at Georgetown University. Given Leroy's gentle demeanor, I suspect I got the better of the argument in the car on the way to Cambridge, but I hope Leroy finds some satisfaction in knowing that I now believe what he believed, even if he may have some uncertainties about what he once believed.

---

[29] "Willie Walker," or that is what we called it around Yale Divinity School, was the text used in Church History classes at Yale. Since I did not want to "waste" my time taking church history, I just read the book and tested out of the course. That may explain why I failed to see the significance that Walker, or at least those who revised Walker's often used textbook, gave to the Anabaptists. Of course, "significance" may be too strong a word in a book that seemed determined to report just "the facts."

But at least Leroy (and the Vietnam war) had gotten my attention. I was busy, of course, writing about character and sanctification, so I did not think I had any reason to try to solve the ethical problems about war in general and the Vietnam war in particular. After all, I was a student at Yale, where we were taught to think critically about convictions even if we discovered we did not have any convictions of our own. Sometime during my last years at Yale, perhaps when I was finishing my dissertation, I was wandering through the Yale Divinity School Bookstore, which I did once a week or so in an effort to keep up on the "new stuff" coming out. My eye fell on a pamphlet entitled *Karl Barth and Christian Pacifism* by someone called John H. Yoder—by this time I had forgotten Leroy had mentioned Yoder to me.[30] Since Barth played a major role in my dissertation, and the pamphlet only cost a dollar (the paper was cheap and the "printing" was just a step above mimeograph), I bought it.

I do not remember when I read Yoder's account of Barth's ethics, but I remember very clearly my reaction to Yoder's presentation of Barth. I thought, "That is the best critique of Barth's ethics I have ever read, but you would have to be crazy to accept Yoder's ecclesiology." He was, after all, a "sectarian." Even though Yoder's account and critique of Barth's understanding of the *Grenzfall* was analogous to the criticisms I had developed in my dissertation concerning Barth's occasionalism, I had no reason to think I should find out anything more about Yoder as I went to teach at Augustana College in Rock Island, Illinois. I thought that being a Methodist sanctificationist was quite enough challenge to the Lutherans at Augie.

---

[30] John's pamphlet was identified as "Work Paper No. 4." Marlin Miller wrote a "Foreword" for the 1966 version although John had written two prefaces, one from Basel, May 7, 1957 and the other from Basel, July 16, 1957. Michael Cartwright told me a story that Al Meyer told him about Yoder having given Barth a copy of his essay on Barth. That led Barth to say to Yoder (and Al): "Oh, Mr. Yoder, you Mennonites are so bellicose." I am not sure how "Work Paper No. 4" found its way into the Yale Divinity Bookstore, but I suspect Jim Gustafson must have had something to do with that. I know Gustafson told me (perhaps at a meeting of the Society of Christian Ethics) that he was trying to get the book published in the new Abingdon Studies in Christian Ethics series under the title *Karl Barth and the Problem of War* (Nashville: Abingdon, 1970). That John's criticism of Barth was not well known may have been due to Abingdon's decision not to continue that venture.

Of course I managed to alienate the Lutherans, but I was rescued by the Catholics who hired me to teach at Notre Dame. What is important about Notre Dame, however, is that South Bend is close to Elkhart. Sometime during my first summer in South Bend, before I had begun teaching at Notre Dame, I thought it might be a good idea to get to know this Yoder. So I drove over to Goshen, assuming that he taught at Goshen College. I discovered that that was not the case, but in the process I wandered into College Mennonite Church, where I found a rack of pamphlets for twenty-five cents each. So I bought three that had been authored by Yoder: his earlier pamphlet on Barth, his essay on capital punishment, and one on Reinhold Niebuhr.

His criticisms of Reinhold Niebuhr were particularly important for me. I began to realize that I was not only reading the work of an extraordinarily powerful mind, but also that I could not have my account of the virtues and Reinhold Niebuhr, too. Put differently, I began to understand that my "Barthianism," which is just another way of saying my Christology, was incompatible with Niebuhr's project to provide a theological justification of political realism. I had earlier begun to see the inadequacy of Niebuhr's understanding of political realism by reading political theorists such as William Connolly, Robert Paul Wolff, and Ted Lowi. But reading Yoder made me realize that I lacked an ecclesiology that could provide an alternative politics. I simply had to learn more about this Yoder guy.

Soon thereafter, I discovered a journal I did not know existed, the *Mennonite Quarterly Review*, by looking in the periodical index under Yoder's name and finding that he published in this journal. This was in 1970, so *The Original Revolution* had not been published. I think the first essays I read in the *MQR* were "The Otherness of the Church" and "Peace Without Eschatology," both of which made an extraordinary impression on me. I was all the more convinced I had to get to know Yoder. I had somehow learned that Yoder was not at Goshen College, but rather taught at Elkhart. With my usual disregard for academic etiquette, I called John up and asked if I could come see him and he invited me over. Sometime that summer I barged into his office armed with a load of arrogance that only Yale can breed.

I do not remember much about that first encounter except that John was his usual diffident self and certainly did not try to charm me into agreeing with his work. Charm and Yoder are not exactly words that belong together. But I suppose the same might be said about me! John responded to my questions with his well-known exactness, saying no more or less than needed to be said to answer what I am sure he thought were ill-formed queries. Because I did not yet know enough to really talk with John, I finally resorted to the academic game: "So what are you working on now?" He said, "Not anything very significant." He was mainly writing things for Mennonite audiences that would probably not interest me. He added that most of what he was doing remained unpublished.

I allowed (Texans "allow") that I was really interested in anything he was doing. So he went through his shelves and I left with a stack of papers about a foot high. I do not remember everything that was in that stack, but it did contain what we now know as *The Politics of Jesus*. I did not comprehend the significance of what I was reading, but I knew it was different. My problem was that I had been well enough educated at Yale to recognize what an extraordinary argument Yoder was making. I had taken a Christology course with Hans Frei in which we had studied not only the classical Christological debates and confessions, but also the work of some Protestant liberals. I had become, and remained, convinced that Chalcedon was and is normative for how we understand the full reality of Jesus as Israel's Messiah. But I was uneasy with Chalcedon insofar as so-called "high Christologies" threaten to make the life and teachings of Jesus secondary for Christian life and thought. So I read *The Politics of Jesus*, which Yoder claimed was merely a report on the consensus of New Testament scholarship, as an extraordinary Christological proposal.

I began to read everything of John's I could get my hands on. I was particularly impressed by *The Christian Witness to the State*, which I wanted to use in a course I had developed in response to the student rebellion, called Christianity, Ethics and Democratic Society. Discovering that it was out of print, I desperately called the Faith and Life Press to see if I could get a hundred copies. In my first discovery of how community works in the Mennonite world, they were more than pleased to crank up the press to make sure I could get the copies I needed. I remember thinking that there did not seem to be much bureaucracy to get in the way of that decision.

Although I was reading Yoder, I had still not decided that I could really endorse his project. Of course, he did not understand it to be his project. However, I felt I could not treat Yoder as representing merely one more position to fit into a Yale typology. Among the papers Yoder had given me was an early draft of his critique of H. Richard Niebuhr's *Christ and Culture*, an argument I found convincing. My chance to come to terms with Yoder came shortly thereafter when I was asked to do the paper for the yearly "ecumenical" meeting of the departments of theology at Valparaiso University and Notre Dame. I decided to write an essay pulling together what I had learned from Yoder.[31]

I began my presentation by noting that what I was going to do before these Lutherans and Catholics was a genuine ecumenical effort. It featured a Methodist with a doubtful theological background (if you are Methodist you have a doubtful theological background), representing a most Catholic department of theology, reading a paper to a group of Missouri Synod Lutherans and saying that the Anabaptists had been right all along. I said that is was an ecumenical gesture because, by the time I finished, the Catholics and Lutherans would discover how much they had in common—namely, thinking it a very good thing to kill the Anabaptists. And, of course, that is exactly what happened, as the Catholics and the Lutherans joined forces to try to show me why we should not take Yoder seriously. Serious people understand that sometimes you do need to kill somebody. I was not convinced, and the rest, so to speak, is history.

---

[31] I, of course, wanted to get this essay published but I had a hell of a time getting anyone to take it. I sent it to many journals, but no one wanted it. The rejections were often less criticism of my essay and more reactions to Yoder. One critic explicitly said that Yoder represented a pre-Bultmannian attitude toward scripture. I should have realized that these rejections meant that any identification with Yoder was not going to win me friends, but I was too taken with what I was learning and naturally too cantankerous to care. I think the essay was finally published in the *Journal of Theology of South Africa*, but I have never seen a copy of it. I had given it to Jim Childress, who gave it to a colleague at Virginia who was on that journal's board. The latter must have sent it to South Africa. Following Paul Ramsey's advice "to never waste a word," I published the essay in my first collection, *Vision and Virtue: Essays in Christian Ethical Reflection*. The book is now published by Notre Dame (probably out of print), but it was originally published by Fides Press in 1974.

I became a Mennonite camp follower. Now the image of "camp follower" may not be appropriate for anyone pretending to have learned much from the Mennonites, since "camp follower" suggests both a military encampment as well as a lady who makes her living in a manner offensive not only to Mennonites but also to most Christians. However, like a camp follower I do not have an ecclesial home, so I whore after that which I think is faithful to the gospel. I cannot pretend that such a position can be made ecclesially intelligible. My only defense is that God in our time seems to have led many of us to that point.[32] We live in a time when the theological battles that seemed so important and justified Christian divisions simply no longer matter. (Consider, for example, the issue of being a "free will Baptist.") That God has made some ecclesially homeless we can only pray will be the beginning of a unity, as John would put it, from the bottom up.[33] Yet the problem of the military imagery remains.

2. How Being A Pacifist Made Me A Warrior

I had become convinced that Yoder was doing work towards which I could not help but be sympathetic, given my own theological convictions. But I was not yet ready to declare myself a pacifist.[34] I remember clearly the first time I said I was a pacifist—a year later, I think. Robert Wilken had joined the Notre Dame faculty and I had begun to press David Burrell, the new chair of the department, to hire Yoder full time. Wilken, then a deeply committed Lutheran and, even worse, a graduate of the University of Chicago, was giving me a ride to a faculty meeting and asking me

---

[32] *In Good Company: The Church As Polis* (Notre Dame: University of Notre Dame Press, 1995) is my most extended set of reflections on this strange ecclesial anomaly to which God seems to have called some of us.

[33] This is the main point of one of the essays John wrote before he died. It has been published in *Pro Ecclesia* 9/2 (Spring 2000): 165-183.

[34] I give a brief account of this in the "Introduction" to *The Peaceable Kingdom: A Primer in Christian Ethics* (Notre Dame: University of Notre Dame Press, 1983), xv-xxvi. When I reread the "Introduction" for this footnote, I realized that I'm going over some of the same ground I covered in the book. I apologize if I seem to be saying what I said before. It does make me wonder if I am the best reporter of how my thinking has developed. My inability to remember dates is well known.

about Yoder. He had a great respect for what he had read of Yoder's work, but observed that he was unconvinced by Yoder's ecclesiology, in particular, his pacifism. For some reason I blurted out that Wilken was wrong and then I said it: "I am a pacifist."

Of course, I had no idea what I was saying, but Yoder had convinced me that you could not separate Christology and the question of nonviolence. So if I was to be fully Chalcedonian in my Christology, if I was to be fully Trinitarian in my doctrine of God, if I was to trust in God's providential care of creation through the calling of the church, then I had to be a pacifist. I have never regretted having so declared myself even though it has never felt like a decision "I made." Rather I am a pacifist because, given the way Yoder had taught me to think, I could not be anything else.

However, being a pacifist creates an entirely different way of thinking about theology. Of course, it is not just pacifism that does so, but rather the way Yoder teaches us to think about theology as a practice of the church. Indeed, it is a mistake to make pacifism *the* practice that isolates Christians from the many other practices necessary for the life of the church. For example, the obligation of Christians to tell one another the truth, to not lie, requires us to develop skillful modes of speech in order to say no more than needs to be said. I would not pretend that I learned all this from Yoder, but what I learned from Yoder has helped me to see connections I otherwise might have missed.

As I began to write about Yoder—and in a manner that I had learned from him, at least to some extent—I began to be claimed by and to learn more about the world that had created John. I was invited several times to speak at the Associated Mennonite Biblical Seminary, where in 1978 I was given a copy of *Martyrs Mirror* in lieu of an honorarium. Well, that is not quite right. They said I could be paid twenty-five dollars or be given a copy of *Martyrs Mirror*. I was not stupid so I took the book, which had a lovely inscription naming me an "honorary Mennonite." Students from AMBS began to come to Notre Dame and take my courses. In the process I learned from them, from what I was reading, as well as from John that neither he nor his work was universally accepted by other Mennonites. In other words, I quickly learned to distinguish Mennonite reality from Mennonite theology—but then that is a distinction that any good

Mennonite makes. After all, it was from John that I learned to think of Mennonite farm culture as a form of Constantianism.

Yet I also had learned to see, in Mennonite life, habits that I might not have learned to see if my seeing had not been trained by John's work. For example, I learned to see how the lack of money could become a resource that enriches a community as it makes cooperation and agreement necessary for survival. Money or wealth can impoverish by robbing us of our need of one another and of the goods we hold in common—goods as basic as shared tractors. From this perspective, the liberal presumption that a community must find a way to balance the needs of the individual with the needs of the whole community makes no sense once the practices of the community are seen as being more primary than whatever we mean by individual or community. John also taught me to see in Mennonite life that theology had to be understood as just one more practice of a people who have learned that their lives depend on learning how to share their lives.

John probably thought I continued to read more philosophy than was good for me, but then I was not fortunate to have had the philosophical foundation that he had, nor did I—nor do I—possess his extraordinary intelligence. He could never understand my difficulty in learning other languages. I needed to read more in order to learn how to do theology in the apparently effortless manner that I saw in John.

If my "thought" or "scholarship" reflects my encounter with Anabaptist thought, that direction is more clearly exhibited in the "how" than the "what" of my work. In particular, I do not think that theology is "thought" that can be abstracted from the practices of a people. In the current academic world this understanding of theology is obviously problematic. I have tried to develop the polemics needed to gain Yoder a hearing in the university as well as the wider church. John, I suspect, thought I was and am far too "contrary"—but then he did not come, as I did, from the mainstream. If "my work" is understood as but a footnote to Yoder, I will think God has used me well indeed.

John, however, would probably worry about how Mennonites might be influenced by me, since my theological work does not appropriately attend to the actual text of the scripture in the manner that John so wonderfully exemplified in his work. For example, I would love to be able to write a book like *He Came Preaching Peace*, but I simply do not have John's extraordinary knowledge of the Scriptures or his uncanny ability to see the connection between texts.[35] Some readers tell me that my work is "biblical," but being "biblical" is not enough.[36] The text and the words matter, and Yoder knew how to make them matter. I hope someone may soon try to show how Yoder did not simply "use" scripture, but rather how he reasoned scripturally.[37]

This is no small matter. I currently have three Mennonite graduate students: Chris Huebner, Alex Sider, and Peter Dula. They represent different streams in Mennonite life but they are all "well formed" Mennonites. I want the training they receive at Duke to serve the upbuilding of the church. I do not want to hurt them, but all I can do is teach them what I have been taught. Of course they read Yoder, but do Mennonites really need to know that much about Aristotle, Aquinas, MacIntyre, and Milbank in order to do theology in the Anabaptist tradition? Will they pick up bad habits—at least bad habits for Mennonites—from me? I hope not, but all I can do is hope. At the very least I hope as they are "reintegrated" into the Mennonite world, what they have learned will help all of us know better how to survive as people committed to Christian nonviolence and how that commitment shapes how theology should be done.

---

[35] *He Came Preaching Peace* is now available through Wipf and Stock Publishers, 199 West 8th Avenue, Eugene OR.

[36] My book, *Unleashing the Scripture: Freeing the Bible from Captivity to America* (Nashville: Abingdon Press, 1993), has been misunderstood or ignored by most readers. That must be due to my inability to know how to proceed after my attack on *sola scriptura* in the first part of the book. What I did not and do not know how to do was make scriptural arguments in the manner of Yoder and Barth. All I could do in that book was exemplify how the words of scripture matter by providing sermonic examples. Probably few readers have thought it profitable to spend time checking my exegesis. The sermons, if read at all, are not read as my attempt to do scriptural reasoning, but rather as exemplifications of my "position." But Yoder is right in saying that theology has gone wrong when it becomes a position rather than a reading.

[37] Richard Hays certainly began that work with his analysis of Yoder in his *The Moral Vision of the New Testament: A Contemporary Introduction to New Testament Ethics* (San Francisco: Harper/ Collins, 1996), 239-253. Michael Cartwright's account of Yoder's scriptural practice in many ways remains unsurpassed. See Cartwright, "Practices, Politics, and Performance: Toward a Communal Hermeneutic for Christian Ethics" (Ph.D. Diss, Duke University, 1988), 298-405.

3. What Bugs Me About Mennonites

It would be pretentious for me to pontificate about what I do not like about Mennonite theology or Mennonite life, since I obviously do not know that much about either. What I know is Yoder, but I do not know what Yoder knew. Of course, I have read books here and essays there by and about Mennonites, but I certainly do not know Mennonite sources or developments in Mennonite theology over the centuries. Having three Mennonite graduate students is helpful, however, because they make me read what I otherwise would not even know existed. For example, Sider and Dula recently had me read Marpeck's "Judgment and Decision." I was struck by how similar Marpeck is to Yoder, which, of course, gets it backwards. But then that is how I learned it—backwards.

For example, Marpeck comments on who should be avoided:

> But I will have nothing to do with any other sect, faction, or gathering, no matter what they are called in the whole world. I will especially avoid those who use bodily sword, contrary to the patience of Christ, who did not resist any evil and who likewise commands His own not to resist tribulation or evil, in order to rule in the kingdom of Christ. I also avoid those who institute, command, and forbid, therewith to lead and rule the kingdom of Christ. I also avoid those who deny the true divinity, Spirit, Word, and power in Jesus Christ. I avoid those who destroy and deny His natural, earthly humanity which was received from man, of the seed of David, born without man's seed and sin, both of Mary the pure virgin; He was crucified and died a natural earthly death, from which He arose again, and has now seated Himself at the right hand of God. I also avoid those who, living in open sin and gross evil, want to have fellowship in the kingdom of Christ but without true repentance, and I avoid all those who tolerate such a thing. I avoid all who oppose and fight against the words and the truth of Christ. With all such, regardless of what they are called in the world, I will have no part or fellowship in the kingdom of Christ unless they repent.[38]

---

[38]Pilgrim Marpeck, "Judgment and Decision," in *Classics of the Radical Reformation*, eds. Walter Klassen and William Klassen (Scottsdale: Herald Press, 1978), 332.

This may seem an unremarkable passage, but what I find so interesting is Marpeck's list, as well as how it is ordered. The use of the "bodily sword" and the confession that Jesus was fully God and fully man are all part of what makes the body of Christ the body of Christ. Indeed the disavowal of the sword and the confession that Christ is who he said he was are not separable. As I suggested above, I learned from Yoder that the practice of nonviolence must be shaped by Christological convictions. But the items on Marpeck's list are connected in another way that is equally important in terms of the crucial challenges before Mennonite life. Marpeck and Yoder both assume that in spite of Anabaptist dissent, Anabaptists remain in continuity with the church catholic and, in particular, with Christological developments. Yet this presumption as well as its implications are denied by many Anabaptists.

That continuity with Catholic Christianity is often denied by Anabaptists is quite understandable. You seldom find yourself in continuity with those who kill you. Moreover, the very fact that Anabaptists were forced to become "Anabaptist" could not help but underwrite the assumption that Mennonites have to "reinvent" Christianity.[39] Yet the idea that somehow the Mennonites are "starting over" is not only theologically doubtful but particularly dangerous in modernity. Theologically it is simply a mistake to assume that God has ever left the world without a faithful witness. The fact that the church is often a witness against itself is but a testimony to God's care of God's church and world. The crucial issue, of course, is what ecclesiological form is best equipped to tell the story of God's faithful care of the church.

Even though I think Denny Weaver is wrong to argue that the ecumenical creeds are compromised by the Constantinian character of the church that produced them, we are in his debt for raising the issue so forcefully. Indeed I believe the recent discussion initiated by Gerald Schlabach and Ivan Kaufmann between Mennonites and Catholics is an extraordinarily important development. We now have a forum where these questions can be investigated with the kind of thoroughness they deserve.

---

[39]Yoder tried to think through these issues in his more "methodological" reflections about historiography. For example, read his "Anabaptism and History," in *The Priestly Kingdom: Social Ethics As Gospel* (Notre Dame: University of Notre Dame Press, 1984), 123-134.

What makes this development so promising is that it is not a matter of Mennonites *opposing* Catholics, since we have Catholics (such as Mike Baxter) who, without being any less Catholic, represent Anabaptist commitments and Anabaptists (like Schlabach) who, without being less Anabaptist, have deep Catholic sensibilities.[40]

Moreover, it would be a mistake to think that the question of the relation between Mennonites and Catholics is primarily about "doctrine," even the doctrine of the church. As I tried to argue in "Whose Church? Which Future? Whither the Anabaptist Vision?" the challenge facing Anabaptists is to discover the implications of living in a world in which they have won.[41] Constantinianism has been defeated. There is no established church for Anabaptists to oppose. Christianity has become voluntary, but the voluntary-ness constituted by modernity makes it impossible to maintain the disciplines necessary to be nonviolent. As is often the case, the terms of the battles of the past may not prepare us well for the challenges we now face.

To suggest that Mennonites need to reconsider their relation with Catholics may only confirm the presumption by many that my unhappy state as a Methodist tempts me to romanticize Mennonites and Catholics. I cannot pretend to be free of that temptation, but Catholic and Mennonite reality is always a welcome check on any form of such romanticization. For instance, my student Peter Dula, a Yankee fan, has told me that the Amish even play golf in Pennsylvania. (It would, of course, be acceptable if they played baseball!) There is much more at stake in the Mennonite/Catholic interaction than mutual sharing of the other's "insights." The unity of Christ's body I take to be the issue—the "issue" that is also at the heart of what it means to be nonviolent.

---

[40] Gerald Schlabach's "Deuteronomic or Constantinian: What Is the Most Basic Problem for Christian Social Ethics?" is one of the most promising developments for helping us to begin to think through the challenges that confront us. His essay appears in *The Wisdom of the Cross: Essays in Honor of John Howard Yoder*, edited by Hauerwas, Chris Huebner, Harry Huebner, and Mark Nation (Grand Rapids: Eerdmans, 1999), 449-471.

[41] This essay now appears in my *In Good Company: The Church as Polis* (Notre Dame: University of Notre Dame Press, 1995), 65-78; also relevant is my "Storytelling: A Response to 'Mennonites on Hauerwas,'" *Conrad Grebel Review* 13/2 (Spring 1995): 166-173.

However, the word "Catholic" does name a reality that Mennonites desperately need. If I were forced to name any aspect of Mennonite life that I find problematic, it would be how Mennonites worship. Mennonite hymnody is obviously a great resource, but I have found Mennonite liturgy generally to be rationalistic and aesthetically thin. Zwingli's rationalistic tendencies have won. For example, believer's baptism invites presumptions that the baptized must "know what they are doing," which in modernity makes the agent of this act the one being baptized rather than God. My problem with believer's baptism has always been what it does for those we unhappily call the "mentally handicapped." If the issue, as Yoder argues, is the question of the baptized being accountable to the church, I do not see why the profoundly mentally handicapped cannot be baptized and held accountable relative to their gifts for the church. The body into which we are baptized is not the individualized body we think of as "ours," but rather Christ's body.[42]

That same body is what we also receive in the Eucharist. When I taught at Notre Dame I often had Catholics who admired the witness of Mennonites say they did not know how Mennonites sustained their nonviolence with infrequent eucharistic celebration. I would try to defend Mennonite practice by pointing out that Mennonites use eucharistic language, but that language "fits" over the way they think their lives must be lived. I continue to think that is a legitimate response. But I also think the Mennonite practice—or the absence of the practice—threatens to makes Mennonites' lives unintelligible. The Eucharist is not the sacrifice we make to an eternally angry God to try to buy ourselves some time; rather the Eucharist is the good news that God would have us included in Christ's sacrifice for the world so the world may have an alternative to pointless and endless sacrifice.

The celebration of the Eucharist, moreover, cannot be separated from questions regarding the shape of the liturgy as well as who is to preside at the celebration of the Eucharist. Questions of ordination and authority cannot be kept at bay if Mennonites are to undertake any reform of worship, which I hope they will indeed do. The alternatives seem to be

---

[42]For this account of the body see Joel Shuman, *The Body of Compassion: Ethics, Medicine, and the Church* (Boulder: Westview Press, 1999).

ethnic identity or church growth strategies. The former has been tried and found wanting; the latter is too ugly to contemplate. But I want to be clear. I am not suggesting that Mennonites should try to mimic Catholic liturgy. Rather, Mennonites need to consider, in a manner faithful to Mennonite life, why word and table cannot be separated.

When I described myself as a "high church Mennonite" many years ago I was not kidding. I am, after all, a Methodist and heir to that unstable brew that is, at least if we take Wesley seriously, at once evangelical and Catholic. Methodists are, or at least should be, free church sacramentalists as well as sanctificationists. Only God knows whether that finally amounts to a coherent ecclesiology, but it at least helps explain why it makes me so happy that some Mennonites find some of what I do useful. I can only pray that we—Catholics, Methodists, Mennonites—will arrive at the moment when we can only make sense of what God has done with us by sharing our stories.

www.ingramcontent.com/pod-product-compliance
Lightning Source LLC
Chambersburg PA
CBHW022005220426
43663CB00007B/971